I0815873

Decolonizing Language and Other Revolutionary Ideas

Also by Ngũgĩ wa Thiong'o

Birth of a Dream Weaver: A Writer's Awakening

Minutes of Glory: And Other Stories

The Perfect Nine: The Epic of Gĩkuyũ and Mũmbi

Wrestling with the Devil: A Prison Memoir

Decolonizing Language and Other Revolutionary Ideas

Ngũgĩ wa Thiong'o

NEW YORK
LONDON

Published in the United States by The New Press, New York, 2025

Distributed by Two Rivers Distribution

ISBN 978-1-620-97932-7 (hc)
ISBN 978-1-620-97936-5 (ebook)

CIP data is available

The New Press publishes books that promote and enrich public discussion and understanding of the issues vital to our democracy and to a more equitable world. These books are made possible by the enthusiasm of our readers; the support of a committed group of donors, large and small; the collaboration of our many partners in the independent media and the not-for-profit sector; booksellers, who often hand-sell New Press books; librarians; and above all by our authors.

www.thenewpress.com

Composition by Dix Digital Prepress and Design

This book was set in Garamond Premier Pro

Printed in the United States of America

10 9 8 7 6 5 4 3 2 1

Contents

Decolonizing Language and Other Revolutionary Ideas

Part One

Decolonizing Language

1
Decolonizing Education

Since the publication of my book *Decolonizing the Mind* in 1986, I have seen, over the years, increasing global interest in issues of decolonization and the unequal power relationships between languages. In 2018, the same issues took me to Limerick, Munster, Ireland, for a conference celebrating 125 years since the foundation of the Gaelic League in 1893.

The league was dedicated to the revival of Gaelic, or Irish, which, by then, in its own country, had become subordinate to the dominant English. Despite many efforts, including official government support for its revival, Irish is still subordinate to English. More Irish speak and use English than they do Irish. Some of the most iconic Irish writers, like W.B. Yeats and James Joyce, wrote in English, and they are studied as part of the canon of English literature. I cannot conceive of an English department anywhere in the world, including Britain itself, without courses in these writers of Irish origins. They have become some of the greatest contributors to English literature.

This unequal power relationship between the two languages in favor of the English was not always the case. The early English settlers in Ireland, Munster in particular, gravitated toward Irish, because, by all accounts, in the beginnings of English settlement, particularly between the thirteenth and the sixteenth centuries, the Irish language was the more endowed in classical learning. Naturally, those early settlers were drawn to the more vibrant Irish tongue. Their gravitation made sense: Irish was the majority tongue, spoken by those among whom the English planters had settled.

London acted, and beginning with the 1366 Statutes of Kilkenny, it passed edicts aimed at protecting the English language against the subversive encroachment of Irish or Gaelic, reinforcing, by law, the use of English, while literally criminalizing Irish. Among other things, the Kilkenny Statutes threatened to confiscate any lands of any English or any Irish living among them who would use "Irish among themselves, contrary to the ordnance." These policies were given a literary and philosophical rationale by no other than the poet Edmund Spenser, author of *The Faerie Queen* and himself a settler in Munster. In his book *A View of the Present State of Ireland,* published in 1596, he argued that language and naming systems were the best means of bringing about the erasure of Irish memory: "It hath ever been the use of the conqueror to despise the language of the conquered, and to force him by all means to learn his."

The marginal status of Irish in its own land did not come about by some kind of natural evolution of language. Its decline in its own land was brought about through conscious political acts and educational policies.

Ireland, it has been observed, was England's first settler

colony. It became a kind of laboratory for other English settler colonies that followed. And what was true for Ireland and other English colonies was equally so for other colonial systems, whether Spanish, French, or Portuguese, or the Japanese occupation of Korea from 1910 to 1945. It is also true in the case of domestic colonialism, like the Norwegian suppression of the language of Sami people, and variations of the same in other Scandinavian countries. The suppression of the languages of the dominated and the elevation of the language of conquest and domination were integral to the education system, which accompanied conquest and colonial occupation.

Linguistic suppression was not undertaken for the aesthetic joy of doing so. Spenser was clear that the colonization of the Irish language and naming system would make the Irish forget who they were, weaken their resistance, and therefore make it easier for the English to conquer and subdue them. Language conquest, unlike the military form, wherein the victor must subdue the whole population directly, is cheaper and more effective: the conqueror has only to invest in capturing the minds of the elite, who will then spread submission to the rest of the population. The elite become part of the linguistic army of the conqueror.

Because of its centrality in the making of modern Britain, India became, even more than Ireland, a social laboratory, whose results were later exported to other colonies in Asia and Africa. Thomas Babington Macaulay, as a member of the Supreme Council of India from 1834 to 1838, helped reform the colony's education system as well as draw up its penal code; both activities have a special significance. In his famous

1835 "Minutes on Indian Education," Macaulay advocated the replacement of Sanskrit and Persian with English as the language of education in order to form a class of "interpreters between us and the millions whom we govern, a class of persons Indian in blood and color, but English in tastes, in opinions, in morals and in intellect."

Eighty-seven years later, Macaulay's words would be repeated in colonial Kenya by the then British governor, Sir Philip Mitchell. In outlining a policy for English language dominance in African education literally as a moral crusade to supplement the armed crusade against the Kenya Land and Freedom Army, a liberation army the British called Mau Mau, he saw this new language education as bringing about a "civilized state in which the values and standards are to be the values and standards of Britain, in which every one, whatever his origins, has an interest and a part." In 1879, Captain Richard Henry Pratt founded the infamous Carlisle Indian Industrial School in Carlisle, Pennsylvania, where he devised his own variant of the method for Native American children, less than twenty miles across the scenic Susquehanna River from the steps of the state capitol in Harrisburg. In 1892, he summed up the philosophy behind the boarding school: "Kill the Indian in him, and save the man." His education program followed the same colonial pattern: uproot a few from their mother tongue, which is spoken by most of their people, mold them anew in the language of conquest, and then unleash them on the governed masses.

In his book *How Europe Underdeveloped Africa*, Walter Rodney quotes Pierre Foncin, a founder of the Alliance

Française, an institution specifically created in 1883 for the propagation of the national language in the colonies and abroad, as being very clear about the goal of the mission. It was "necessary to attach the colonies to the Metropole by a very solid psychological bond against the day when their progressive emancipation ends in a form of federation as is probable—that they be and they remain French in language, thought and spirit."[1]

The goal was very clear. Imperial educational policies were meant to create colonies of the mind, among the elite of the colonized. The success of these policies is undeniable. A variation of the Irish situation, where even after independence, the intellectuals express themselves more fluently in the language of imperial conquest than in the languages from their own country, is present in every postcolonial situation. In the case of Africa, you even hear the identity of the continent being described in terms of Europhonity: Anglophone, Francophone, and Lusophone, mainly. Even where the elite are nationalistic and assertive of their independence, they find it easier to express their outrage and hopes in the languages of imperial conquest. Ninety percent of the monies allocated for language education goes to pamper imperial languages. Ninety percent of the population still speaks African languages anyway. Some governments even view African languages as enemies of progress. They believe that imperial languages are really the gateway to global modernity.

Under normal circumstances, it would sound odd to hear that French literature can only be written in Japanese, or English literature in IsiZulu, so that when you meet a French writer who writes in French, you look at them in surprise: Why on earth are you writing in French? Or an English writer writing in English: Why are you not writing in Zulu? And yet this absurdity is expected of African writers and writers from those formerly colonized.

How did this absurdity come about? It is not that those languages are more of language than any other. And under any circumstances, to know more languages can only empower the person. But this was not the case in colonial contexts or any context in which there is a dominating and dominated. It was never a case of adding a new language to what one already had. For the colonial conqueror, it was not enough to introduce an additional language to any community. Imperial languages had to be planted on the graveyard of the languages of the dominated. The death of African languages gave life to European languages. In order for the imperial language to be, the language of the colonized had to cease to be. Amnesia for African languages; anamnesis for European languages.

These two conditions are not inherent in the character of the languages involved. They are mental conditions consciously brought about by how the imperial languages were imposed.

In *Decolonizing the Mind*, I have talked about the corporal punishment meted out to African children caught speaking an African language at school, children who were then made to carry a placard around the neck proclaiming their stupidity. In some cases, the culprit was made to swallow filth, thus associating African languages with criminality, pain, and filth. This was not just in Africa.

In his 2015 testimony to the Waitangi Tribunal about his

experiences of school in New Zealand, Dover Samuels, a Maori politician, tells a similar story. Caught speaking Maori in the school, he said, "You'd be hauled out in front of the rest of the class . . . and told to bend over. . . . You'd bend over and he'd stand back and give you, what they called it then, six of the best. . . . On many occasions, not only did it leave bruises behind on my thighs but drew blood."[2]

The Sami people in Norway went through a similar experience in the period between 1870 and 1970—what they call the brutal century—in an attempt to turn them into fluent Norwegian-language speakers.

Similar violence against native languages is the running theme in the spread of English in the rest of Ireland and in Scotland and Wales. In Wales those who spoke Welsh in the school compound were made to stand in front of the class, with a placard reading WELSH NOT hanging from their neck.

Violence was central in creating the psychological bond of language, culture, and thought: colonies of the mind. You would think that after liberation and independence, the new nations, at the very least, would dismantle that unequal power relationship. But that is precisely the power of the colonies of the mind: negativity toward self has become internalized as a way of looking at reality.

It is a classic case of conditioning you will find in manuals of behavioral psychology. Conditioning is a system of reward and punishment, punishment for undesired behavior and reward for the desired behavior. It is often used in various degrees of intensity in bringing up children or taming animals. The undesired behavior becomes associated with punishment, and hence pain; the desired behavior, with reward, and hence pleasure. The object of conditioning, a child or an animal, comes to automatically avoid the space of pain, the forbidden behavior, and gravitate toward the space of pleasure, the required behavior. In the case of learning, one became the recipient of glory for excelling in the language of conquest, but the recipient of a gory mess for uttering even a single word in one's mother tongue. One's mother tongue became the space of pain, to be avoided, and the conquering language becomes the space of pleasure, to be desired.

In the end, the conditioned develop a Pavlovian consciousness, wherein even the sound associated with rewards or punishment can make the mouth water in anticipation of pleasure or make the mouth dry up at the prospect of pain. The trauma experienced by the first generation of the conditioned can be passed on as normal behavior that needs no explanation or justification; the later generations may not even understand why they associate pain with native and pleasure with foreign languages and cultures. In the case of language, the elite and educational planners of the formerly colonized societies assume that European (imperial) languages are inherently global and best able to carry intelligence and universality. That assumption may also explain why criminalizing African languages continues to this day, now administered and enforced by African educationists who don't see the irony of what they are doing: an African punishing another African for speaking an African language, by order of an African government.

The trauma initially wrought by the colonial education

system is thus passed on, inherited. Abnormality becomes normalized. The normalized abnormality is nationalized as the desirable goal of education.

The colony of the mind prevents meaningful, nationally empowering innovations in education. The control by the colonizer of the colonized is inherent in the inequality of the education system. Education may become a process of mystifying the cognitive process and even knowledge.

Here we need to make a distinction between education and knowledge. Knowledge is a question of continuously adding to what we already know in a dialectical play of mutual impact and illumination. The normal cognitive process starts from the known and heads toward the unknown. Every new step makes more of the unknown known and therefore adds to what is already known. The new known enriches the already known, and so on, in a continuous journey of making dialectically related connections. Knowledge of the world begins where one is.

Education, on the other hand, is a mode of conditioning people to make them fit into, and function in, a given society. It may involve transference of knowledge, but it is conditioned knowledge, branded by the world outlook of the educator and the education system. A careful study of the colonial process, as a particular instance of the dominant and the dominated, the master and the servant, can be useful in thinking about balanced and inclusive education. Colonial education was never balanced or inclusive. It has been a question of drawing lessons from the negative.

The colonial process was always a negation of the normal

cognitive process. Imperial Europe—its names, its geography, its history, its knowledge—was always seen as the starting point of the educational journey of the colonized. In short, colonization, in the area of education, was always predicated on the negation of the colonized space as the starting point of knowledge. In the area of language, it meant a negation of native languages as valid sources of knowledge and means of intellectual and artistic inquiry. The lack of roots in our base creates a state of permanent uncertainty about our relationship to where we are, to our abilities, even to our achievements.

Decolonization must be at the heart of any balanced and inclusive education. Both the formerly colonizing and the formerly colonized are affected by the colonial system that has shaped the globe over the last four hundred years. Decolonization has to mean the negation of the negation mandated by colonization. Knowledge starts wherever we are. Our languages are valid sources of knowledge. We all love the stars, but we don't have to migrate to Europe, physically or metaphorically, in order to reach them.

In the case of languages, we have to reject the commonly held wisdom that the problem in any one country or the world is the existence of many languages and cultures, and even religions. The problem is their relationship in terms of hierarchy. My language is higher in the hierarchy than yours. My culture is higher than yours. Or my language is global; yours is local. And in order for you to know my language, you must first give up yours. The view that my god is more of a god than your god is very ungodly. This view leads some people to see their own language as inherently more of a language than other languages and therefore to insist that they themselves must be ranked higher in knowledge and power. This is what I call linguistic feudalism.

All languages, large and small, have a lot to contribute to our common humanity if freed from linguistic feudalism. Education policies should be devised on the basis that all languages are treasuries of history, beauty, and possibility. They have something to give to one another if their relationship is that of the give-and-take of a network. Even if one of the languages emerges as the language of communication across many languages, it should not be so on the basis of its assumed inherent nation-ness or globality, but on the basis of need and necessity. And even then, it should *not* grow on the graveyard of other languages.

Balanced and inclusive education calls for a new slogan: Network, not hierarchy. We have to understand that all languages, big and small, have a common language: it is called translation.

Education should never lead to linguistic and cultural self-isolation. I want to connect to the world, but I don't have to negate my starting base first. I want to connect to the world from wherever I am. I believe that the goal of education is knowledge that empowers, that shows our real connections to the world, but from our base. From our base we explore the world: from the world we bring back that which enriches our base.

That, it seems to me, is the real challenge in organizing knowledge and transmitting it in an inclusive and balanced education system in the world today. We have to reject the notion that:

Splendor is not splendor unless it springs from squalor.
Palaces are not palaces unless erected on prisons.
My millions are not millions unless mined from a
 million poor.
For me to be, others must cease to be.

Education must convey knowledge that empowers us to imagine more inclusive palaces, where my being enables your being and yours enables mine.

2

The Body of Knowledge

The process of knowing is simple. No matter where you want to journey, you start from where you are. If you are in Nairobi and you want to go to Nakuru, you don't first go to Mombasa to start your journey to Nakuru. The same with knowledge. Our knowledge of the world and the universe begins with our bodies.

The body is the primary field of knowledge and production. The five-fingered hand is the natural maker of things. It is a natural technology. Some of the most complex technologies are a projection of the human hand. The leg is the primary enabler of movement from one location to another. Every technology of transport, from skateboards, bicycles, and motorcars to airplanes, rockets, and spaceships are, in some way, a projection of the leg. In the same way, all technologies of seeing—from a pair of glasses and a magnifying glass to the finest telescope—are an extention of the eye. The technologies of listening and hearing are derived from the ear. The last frontier is the human brain. The human brain is a natural computer, our squishy hard drive. With its capacity to store, recall, and transmit memory in time, computer technonology is replicating and enhancing the natural properties of the human brain. Imagination is the only human attribute that cannot as yet be replicated by technologies. And without imagination, there would be no science, no architecture, no technology, no invention, no innovation, among other things. Technology is first developed in imagination before it becomes a fact.

"What is now proved was once, only imagin'd," writes William Blake, in his *Marriage of Heaven and Hell.*

Imagination coupled with these other natural technologies constitutes this awesome being, the human body, which interacts with the immediate environnment—the earth, the water, the air, and also life in the form of plants and animals, as well as all the resources of the earth—to make things. That is why the human body has been the site of struggle between contending social forces, within nations or between nations.

We can see this in conquest and colonization. The first blow to Africa came when the Black body was enslaved and taken to a new environment in order to produce for another. The second blow was colonialism. Here the body was made to work on the home environment, with all the natural resources that used to belong to it, but now it works for another. The colonized planted; the colonizer harvested.

At the same time, the colonizers wanted the colonized to believe that they, the overlords, were the source of the knowledge and power that made production possible. Here the first psychological blow was, quite literally, the act of demeaning their bodies, then their minds. The aim was to make them question themselves, to destabilize their relationship to their own bodies and minds, to un-know what they were capable of doing. This literal depression of the conquered went together with the elevation of the mind and body of the conqueror. The outsiders depicted themselves as the owners of technology, invention, and innovation. They tried to convince the conquered Other that, without the conquerors' technologies, there would be no production beyond foraging for fruit or hunting animals with their bare hands. I remember some teachers in my colonial school saying that Africa never invented the wheel.

Don't get me wrong. There were areas in which the newcomers had superior technology, for example, warfare: the arrow, though superior to the spear, was no match for the gun that spewed death through fire and smoke. Technology has always developed and spread unevenly in different cultures and histories, as people have borrowed or stolen from one another. But the capacity to make things, to innovate, is thoroughly human, not the monopoly of any one race, culture, or history. Certainly Africa was not an unchanging society of peoples who lived by hunting and gathering. Africans planted and even domesticated animals.

Two essential parts of precolonial African architecture were the kraal, where goats and cows were housed at night, and the granary, where harvests were stored. The cow and the goat ensured milk and leather clothes and goods; a full granary ensured food for the family at all times, certainly so until the next harvest. But in addition to those who produced food, there were those who worked in metal in their little factories, *iganda*, as the Gĩkũyũ people called them, producing metal arrowheads, spears, machetes, and axes—tools for the dual struggle with nature and other human groups. There were also factories for pottery, not to mention those who made cloths out of materials like the bark of trees. It cannot be overemphasized that it was the African who built those marvels of ancient Egypt and those of the medieval city Great Zimbabwe, not forgetting those wonderful earth structures in West Africa or those magnificent Ethiopian cathedrals hewn out of rock.

However, to normalize the perception of the outsider as the bringer of technology and innovation, and most important, to make the colonial subject accept that view, the colonizers had to erase the memory of what had been. History books erased the fact that Egyptian or Ethiopian technologies originated in Africa, in the black body. They attributed the construction of Great Zimbabwe or the Egyptian pyramids to some light-skinned people from nowhere.

By many strokes of many pens, the intellectual architects of enslavement and colonialism erased Africa's contributions to technology and innovation from the history books. You remember Hume, that doyen of European en-nightenment? In his *Treatise on Human Nature*, he could not find any individual among Black people who was eminent either in action or speculation: "No ingenious manufactures amongst them, no arts, no sciences."

You will find similar thoughts among other eminent thinkers, including Immanuel Kant and Georg Wilhelm Friedrich Hegel. Hegel emphatically declared that history, as the embodiment of enlightenment, of reason and science, had bypassed Africa, which remained enveloped in the dark mantle of the night, an image no doubt arising from his reading of colonial travel narratives that talked about Dark Africa or Darkest Africa. Hegel's image becomes a truth in the grandiloquent stupidity of Oxford University's Hugh Trevor-Roper, who in the 1960s claimed that Africa had only darkness to exhibit prior to European colonial presence. Since darkness was not a subject of history, the history of Africa began with European colonization.

The twin forces of slaving and colonizing did not stop at literary erasure. As Walter Rodney argued in *How Europe Underdeveloped Africa*, they also destroyed the African artisan class as independent producers.

The demise of the artisans had other consequences. Knowledge, information and its interpretation, is normally passed from one generation to the next. All make improvements from their own experience and from the challenges of making things, or from comparisons between how and what they make and how and what things are made elsewhere. Borrowing from others has always been a necessary addition to the inherited, a source of improvement. They both create a tradition. The destruction of the native class of artisans meant the end of living teachers, the end of a tradition, and also the end of the memory of the possible.

Some of you may have come across relatives or neighbors who have lost their memory, through either senility or a traumatic experience. They simply cannot connect anything to anything. They don't even remember their own children and relatives or their past interactions with them. They have no stable reference point. To a smaller or greater degree, an entire people can also suffer the collective loss of memory. I am sure there are members of the young generation who don't believe that the soldiers of the Kenya Land and Freedom Army, otherwise known as Mau Mau, made guns in their factories in the mountains.

Colonial education and related practices tried to induce collective amnesia about Africa, about its technology and innovation. Even if acknowledged—as in the case of Benin sculptures, which decisively influenced Picasso and the European modernist movement—such artistic products are often condemned as designs of the devil. Through collective amnesia, induced or not, it is possible to forget that Africa ever made things.

The next logical step is to see the outsider as the sole source of knowledge, technology, and innovation. So you hear: *Mzungu hapana cheza na yeye.* A recurring image in one of my plays, *Mother, Sing for Me*, represents an attempt by some characters to challenge this "Mzungu can do anything" nonsense. Every time a character tries to demonstrate that African people can make things—guns, for instance—he is stopped by the colonial plantation owner, and his hands are amputated. In the play, after a long struggle, the plantation is eventually managed by African directors, and the workers once again show that they have the skills to make weapons. Unfortunately, they meet the same fate: amputation of their arms so they can never try making "arms" again. In addition, their tongues are removed so that they can never pass their knowledge on to the next generation. The play was really talking about the African capacity for technology and innovation, and how it has been consciously thwarted. The play was in Gĩkũyũ, and it was banned in 1982.

The *hapana-cheza-na-Mzungu* business was reinforced by the subordination of native languages to that of the outsider. The language of a region holds the most effective and wide-ranging knowledge of the environment of that particular region. Destroy a people's language, and you destroy the vocabulary by which they understood their environment, and consequently all the knowledge and information developed in the course of their interactions with that environment.

The language of the outsider becomes the language of power and normality. The vocabulary by which the conquering outsider looks at the conquered, their history, their productive capacities, is that of the outsider. The colonial education system, enforced by the colonial language, was imbued through and through with the worldview of the outsider looking in. Those who went to the colonial school can remember that lessons in geography and history started with those of Europe.

The educated African may have consciously or unconsciously come to adopt the view of the outsider looking in. And in postcolonial Africa, the European language–educated elite has normalized the viewing of Africa from outside itself. This result, an educated African middle class looking at their own countries and histories as if they themselves stood outside both, was intended. All colonial powers had discovered the economic utility of educating the African elite in the image of the West. Indeed, it has come to pass that intellectual production in Africa today is always in European languages, which means that we shall always look at Africa with the language of the outsider.

This externalizing has several consequences. The colonial outsider always saw knowledge as coming from outside. The African inheritors of that tradition come to view Africa in the same way: Africa cannot be a real source of technology and innovation. Or what is produced within is not as good as what is made abroad. Or whatever is produced within must first be validated by Europe and the West.

Today, where are the Africans who make things out of the raw material around them and then exchange the surplus in local, national, continental, or world markets? Africa produces gold, diamonds, copper, uranium, and oil, and yet if you visit the capitals of the regions where these raw materials are abundant, you will not find a thriving industry rooted in the mines. Given our precolonial history, are there any reasons why we Kenyans or other Africans cannot do what China is doing today, prospering as a workshop for the world? If precolonial Africans, using rock, could explore the astronomical universe before Stonehenge, is there any reason that today's Africans cannot lead us in space—or at the very least become an equal partner in such explorations and discoveries? We can feed ourselves, clothe ourselves, house ourselves, and build new wonders for ourselves through the kind of creative interactions with our environment that colonialism and corporate imperialism have alienated us from.

One of the dire consequences of the outsider looking in is

the development of a looting mentality. With the economy of the colony integrated to that of the mother country, Africa became a looter's paradise for the settler. The colonial state—the police, the army, the law, the bureaucracy—was a vehicle for more effective looting. The educated, European language–speaking African elite inherited and internalized the outsider's view of the continent, and also the looting mentality that went with it.

To put it simply, when you don't feel you own a country, you probably won't feel accountable for its state of affairs. People don't normally rob themselves. Instead, they take care of their own property and try to ensure its protection. Corruption is stealing from the people of Kenya and all Africa, and it is driven by the mentality of the outsider looking in. This was the main theme in my novel *Devil on the Cross*, which I wrote in Kamĩtĩ Maximum Security Prison in 1978. In the novel, I depicted a competition organized by the devil to choose the seven cleverest robbers. But these are no ordinary robbers: to qualify for the competition, one must demonstrate that one has robbed millions or billions from the people. These are world-class thieves. They testify to their past heroic plundering, but they also articulate a vision of future theft. The winner will be crowned Chief of Robbers by the Organization for Modern Theft and Robbery, then headquartered in New York. I would recommend the book to all those who desire a resurgent Africa.

The rampant corruption that permeates most of Africa is rooted in viewing our continent with the eyes of the outsider. We can reverse this. Earlier I said that the performance of the

Gĩkũyũ-language play *Maitũ Njugĩra*, or *Mother, Sing for Me*, was banned in 1982. I have always believed that it was banned, as was an earlier play that I co-wrote, *Ngaahika Ndeenda* (*I Will Marry When I Want*), because the Kamĩrĩthũ effort showed a vision of a new Kenya of self-reliance in education, technology, and innovation, a new Kenya rooted in the power of Kenyan people. The play remained banned for over thirty years, until 2015, when President Uhuru Kenyatta, at the opening ceremony of the refurbished National Theater, revoked the ban. I saw hopeful symbolism in the act, even though it took the action of a president who has publicly embraced innovation to unban a play that thirty-three years earlier was celebrating the capacity and potential of Kenyans for technology and innovation.

I believe that the modern university in Kenya and, more broadly, in Africa can open the way to our future as a modern nation and continent. However, such a university must believe that knowledge begins where we are. I am talking of a cognitive process built on the principle of "from our base to the world" and not the other way round.

In 1968, the late Owuor Anyumba, Taban Lo Liyong, and I challenged the dominance of English literature at the University of Nairobi. It is not that we disliked English literature, or thought any less of its greatness, but we objected to the way it took center stage in the teaching of literature. We called for the abolition of the English Department as then organized with British literature as the center. We called for renaming it the Department of Literature, with African, Caribbean, African American, Asian, and Latin American literatures as its center, alongside European literature, in that order. The debate, the reorganization, and the new outlook would later launch postcolonial studies and postcolonial theory throughout the world. From Nairobi we conversed with the world.

I believe that this principle works in the areas of economy, politics, and innovation. But only by drawing from our strength and faith as Kenyan people can we propel our country to the forefront among the nations of the Earth. That calls for the end of the colonially inherited mentality of looking at Kenya and Africa as a looter's paradise. Nobody ever robs their own house. Nobody would ever willingly let others rob their house, much less partner with others to do so.

From Kenya to the world. From Kenya to the stars. That should be the slogan of our institutions of higher learning. Reach for the stars. Even better, become a star. Thus help light the way for our country, our nation, Africa, and the world.

3
Between Enslavement and Empowerment

Every society has had its intellectuals, and they are not a new creation in Africa, here defined as workers in ideas. They may do other things, but their primary social significance and visibility was as workers in ideas. African healers, seers, and artisans, including builders, were in this category. Intellectuals were an integral part of the old Egyptian, Ethiopic, Zimbabwean, and Soghai civilizations.

A most important component of this precolonial intellectual class was the poet, who often combined the roles of historian, moralist, and seer. In West Africa, they call him the griot. Swahili civilization is replete with poets, leaders of thought spanning centuries. A book edited by Abdilatif Abadalla and published by Mkuki na Nyota, *Kale ya Washairi wa Pemba* (The Past of Pemba Poets), lists quite a few, including Fumo Liyongo wa Baury in the twelfth century, Muyaka bin Haji al-Ghassaniy in the eighteenth century, and Suud-bin Said Al-Maamiriy in the nineteenth century. These poet-intellectuals largely saw themselves as the voices of the people and seekers of justice. It may seem needless to say, but it is important to emphasize that these intellectuals, from Egyptian to Ungozi/Uswahili times, used the languages of their society. Precolonial African intellectuals were rooted in their own communities.

I want to focus on the *modern* African intellectual. I am talking, of course, of the intellectual who has been to a modern school and for whom European languages have been the means of their education. There have been two faces and phases of this African intellectual, and these phases are almost contradictory.

The intellectuals of the anticolonial struggle used European languages to get what they carried and then took it back to African languages to enrich them. They explored European languages as scouts.

In the Gold Coast, which is today Ghana, a statement published in *The Gold Coast People* of November 30, 1893, called upon the Fante intellectuals of the time to be thankful that the "Fantis are proud to be Fantis and are not ashamed to be known by their native names, heard speaking their liquid language, and seen arrayed in their flowing robes."[1] In a nutshell, "Instead of Europeanized Africans, they wanted to become native civilized Africans."[2]

Similar sentiments were expressed by nineteenth-century South African black intellectuals emerging from the Lovedale Mission.

In East Africa we have the example of Shaaban bin Robert with his famous poetic quip about scales of values: *Titi la Mama litamu lingawa la Mbwa, lingine halishi tamu.* "Mother's milk is sweeter than a dog's, but a dog's is still sweet."

Upon Ghana's independence in 1957, Kwame Nkrumah moved quickly to establish an African language bureau. He helped train teachers to teach African languages. He established newspapers in African languages. In his opening address to the First International Conference of Africanists in Accra in 1962, he hoped that the gathering would be a major step toward an Africa-centered view of itself, its history and culture, with African languages at the center.

He came back to the same theme when a year later he opened the first Institute of African Studies. For him the study and development of African languages was not a side issue. African languages were central to African scholarship and development, and to Africans' relationship with the diaspora and the world. The key thing is that he put resources into his commitment. Alas, the military coups that followed reversed his policy, with some cheering from the Ghana middle class.

The anticolonial struggle in Kenya gave rise to a vigorous nationalist press in African languages. Jomo Kenyatta was once editor of an African-language paper, *Mũigwithania* (The Unifier). Later he wrote a book called *Kenya Bũrũri wa Ngũĩ* (Kenya, the Land of Conflicts). This was in addition to his famous book, *Facing Mount Kenya*, in English. As part of its war machine, the colonial state banned the African-language press, forcing some editors into exile and others into prison.

At Tanzania's independence in 1961, Kambarage Nyerere established Swahili as the national language. At long last, Kiswahili had a home. Nyerere translated Shakespeare into Kiswahili. He led by example, giving some of his major speeches in Kiswahili or having his works translated into Kiswahili.

These intellectuals used their access to English for self-empowerment.

This was very different from the post-independence African middle class, which holds the reigns of power; they became captives of European languages. Some years ago, in independent Kenya, parliament voted to ban African languages in official premises. The irony was that this parliament was possible only because an African language–speaking working class had organized in the mountains and in the streets to oust the British colonial state. The parliament did not see itself rooted in an African-language past but in that of English and other European languages. This ban is not yet law only because the president has never signed it into law.

Language has always been a battlefield of ideas. It is a war zone in the struggle between enslavement and empowerment, between the dominated and the dominating, the colonized and the colonizing. The history of a language, Tom Paulin has written, is often a story of possession and dispossession, territorial struggle, and the establishment or imposition of a culture. Language has been as much the tool of conquest and resistance as the sword. Indeed some of the fiercest battles have been fought and continue to be fought in this zone. Not that language is the prime mover, but it is often seen as a necessary consequence of conquest, the element needed to cement conquest.

After their conquest of Africa, the French, British, and Portuguese did not actually ban African languages and naming systems; they marginalized them as languages of power, knowledge, and identity. Even where they allowed African languages in the education system, it was only as a first step before the students were turned into English and French speakers. I am not aware of any law banning African names in the continent, but through cultural engineering, the Gramscian hegemony of culture, every educated African today appends a European name, however ridiculous or ill-fitting, to his African name. The colonial language policies were a continuation of war by linguistic means.

The African continent continues to suffer the consequences of linguistic conquest. Political independence may have freed the body, but it certainly did not free the mind. This is the long-term effect of linguistic domination.

The result for Africa is a gigantic disconnect between the educated middle class and the general population, which was always the intention of the colonial enterprise. If you think of languages in terms of war, it was as if the African generals became captives in the enemies' camp. By generals I don't just mean the government alone. I am thinking of the entire intellectual class; none of us can say we have escaped the consequences of our acceptance of defeat or our attempts to lead the intellectual and academic battles as captives.

As captives, we are forced to look at the continent as if we are outsiders. Our various fields of knowledge of Africa are in many ways rooted in that entire colonial tradition of the outsider looking in, gathering and coding knowledge with the help of native informants, and then storing the final product in a European language for consumption by those who have access to the acquired tongue. Today, we still collect intellectual items and put them in European language museums and archives.

The intellectual community inside and outside Africa has come to accept this as the norm.

At a conference at Leeds University attended by more than five hundred scholars from Africa and Europe, I posed this question: How many of the scholars present had ever written a single document in an African language? Not a hand was raised when it came to books. Not a hand was raised when it came to even a single paper. When it came down to a page, three hands were raised—three hands at a conference of top-notch scholars and experts on Africa. I have posed similar questions in Nigeria and Kenya before a predominantly African audience. The results were similar.

Perhaps my point would be clearer if we posed the question the other way: Can you think of a professor of Italian history or culture who does not know a word of Italian? Or a professor of French history who did not have a word of French? A professor of Greek and Latin without Latin and Greek? Abnormal, you would say; but the abnormal and even the ridiculous have become the norm for the largest continent in the world, larger than all Europe, the Americas, and China put together.

Surely this has to change, and this change can only come about as a result of cooperation among an academy that is willing to countenance other ways of knowing, publishers who are willing to countenance other ways of publishing, and intellectuals who are willing to put in the necessary effort. But another partner is necessary: governments with pro-African language policies.

However, we should remember that the people who run

those governments are also products of the academy. Perhaps if their orthodoxy about governance had been challenged at the academy, when they were students, they might have emerged as generals instead of captives, as free agents willing to find other ways of fighting and knowing. But little can change when governments are under enormous pressure to operate within the boundaries of conquest and defeat.

There are tiny glimpses of hope that things may be turning round. Kiswahili is at the forefront. The triumph of Kiswahili in Tanzania is the result of the intellectuals of the first type—those who got from European languages whatever they had and stored the positive in an African language. I have already mentioned Nyerere, who was a graduate of two of the leading institutions of the time—Makerere and then Edinburgh—and used his knowledge of Shakespeare, acquired in English, to translate the work of the bard into Kiswahili. He also empowered Kiswahili through active pro-Kiswahili policies and resources. The limitation was in the assumption that a national language can only be built on the graveyard of other African languages. Monolingualism, as synonymous with the nation-state, is rooted in the European idea of the nation-state, which, ironically, was forged at the beginnings of the modern capitalist and colonial enterprise in the seventeenth century.

Not surprisingly, Tanzania has also produced a publisher who has been very consistent in his commitment to publishing in African languages, mostly Kiswahili. Walter Bgoya's Mkuki na Nyota has not only revived Swahili classics, but also generated new writers. Henry Chakava of East African Educational Publishers has also brought out the Kiswahili translations of nearly all the major African writers in English and French.

But is the academy as a whole following suit?

Even here are glimpses of hope. A small step, though giant in its potential, has been taken in the area of philosophy in the book *Listening to Ourselves,* edited by the Caribbean-Canadian intellectual Chike Jeffers and published by the State University of New York Press. The book contains essays on philosophy in several African languages: Wolof, Dholuo, Igbo, Akan, Amharic, Gĩgĩkũyũ, and Luo, with English translations. The contributors, who include the late Emmanuel Eze, are some of the leading African scholars in philosophy, holding professorial ranks at universities inside and outside Africa. As far as I know, this is the first time I have come across pieces written by modern African philosophers in African languages. In my foreword to the book, I commended Jeffers for laying to rest "the questions as to whether written modern philosophy is possible in African languages."

It has taken a person of Caribbean origins to do a first for Africa. Even within the limitations of a Western academy, he is doing what should have been common practice in Africa. It has been his dream to do this; thus he takes his place in a long line of others who have dreamed and acted for Africa: Marcus Garvey, C.L.R. James, George Padmore, W.E.B. Du Bois, and Walter Rodney, to cite a few.

Jeffers's work points to yet another language that has not been widely used in a conscious way to empower African languages. Translation, I have argued in my book *Something*

Torn and New, is the language of languages. There is hardly any culture that has not gained from translation. Translation between African languages and translation between African languages and other languages of the world would be a win-win situation for Africa and world cultures. Our colleges and universities should be beehives of translation from other languages into African languages. Nyerere showed the way.

All this calls for a grand alliance of scholars, academies, publishers, and educational policymakers. Intellectuals inside and outside Africa must lead: they have to live up to their venerable tradition. The intellectual in all cultures and histories has been a pathfinder, and in all cultures, these intellectuals have had to pay a price, sometimes with their own lives. I have had to pay a price, not too big a price, but a price all the same: prison, exile even. The intellectuals of our times must not run away from the fight, from the zones of war.

Moreover, governments and institutions cannot continue to hide their heads in the sand of globalization. Globalization began with the black body, back in the seventeenth century in the slave trade and then on the plantation. Plantation slavery mutated into colonialism. Globalization today is dependent on resources still available in Africa. Many governments, academics, and intellectuals have the illusion that globalization demands that they get lost in English. They should remember this: the Brits gave us our English accent. We gave them their African access. In the seventeenth and eighteenth centuries, it was their access to the black body; in the nineteenth and twentieth centuries, it was their access to copper, gold, diamonds, and now oil. Today while we are very busy perfecting our English, they are very busy perfecting their pipeline to the resources of the continent.

It's time we spent more time perfecting all the means at our disposal to protect the wealth of Africa. Languages are part of the fight. Remember Shaaban bin Robert: *Titi la Mama litamu . . . , lingine halishi tamu*. Mother tongue is best, always.

4
The Magic Fountain

Eric Ashby's book *African Universities and Western Tradition* collects the Godkin Lectures he gave at Harvard University in 1964. It was the year I graduated from Makerere College with a University of London honors degree in English. The same year, William Heinemann brought out a hardcover edition of my novel *Weep Not, Child*, written in English, obviously a product of my five years at Makerere. My novel and I were products of the kind of universities that Eric Ashby was talking about, whose social function was "to produce men and women with the standards of public service and capacity for leadership which self-rule requires"—in short, a governing elite in the expected new political dispensation following the end of the Second World War.

The colleges were established in the fifties, the culmination of a series of committees and recommendations going back to the 1925 Advisory Committee on Education in the Colonies, which years later morphed into the Asquith Colonial Higher Education Commission and the Inter-University Council for Higher Education Overseas.

However, the vision of a modern university in Africa did not begin in the twentieth century with these official committees, but rather in the nineteenth century with James Africanus Beale Horton in 1868 and Edward Blyden in 1872.

Horton and Blyden were of African descent, both from Sierra Leone, and they clearly wanted the best for Africa. Nevertheless, their two visions were different. According to Eric Ashby, Horton wanted to introduce into Africa an "undiluted Western education," and "there was no place in his scheme of higher education for the incorporation of African languages, history or culture." The way to African modernity lay in the Greek classics and European languages and cultures. Blyden, on the other hand, wanted to free higher education in Africa from "despotic Europeanizing which had warped and crushed the Negro mind."

Writing in 1883, Blyden said:

> All our traditions and experiences are connected with a foreign race. We have no poetry but that of our taskmasters. The songs which live in our ears and are often on our lips are the songs we heard sung by those who shouted while we groaned and lamented. They sung of their history which was the history of our degradation. They recited their triumphs which contained the record of our humiliation. To our great misfortune, we learned their prejudices and their passions, and thought that we had their aspirations and their power.

Blyden envisioned a system of education that rejected all the errors and falsehoods about the African, and while the Greek and Latin classics would be part of the curriculum for his African university, he also wanted African languages to be an integral part of it.

J.E. Casely Hayford of Ghana, then Gold Coast, was to go further than Blyden. In his *Ethiopia Unbound* of 1911, he, too, articulated a vision of an African university in which the medium of instruction would be an African language, and to meet the needs of the relevant material, scholars would be employed to translate books into African languages.

When eventually universities were set up in Africa following the recommendations of the Asquith committee—the University of Ibadan in 1948, the University College of the Gold Coast (now the University of Ghana) in 1948, Makerere University College in 1950—it was the Horton vision that triumphed, except that where Greek and Latin had earlier been the foundation of excellence, English took over as that foundation. I shall call this the Horton-Asquith model to contrast it with that of Blyden and Casely Hayford.

Horton and Asquith differed from Blyden and Casely Hayford not about the need for excellence in higher education but rather the way of achieving it. The question of African languages was thus central to the two models. In the Horton-Asquith model, African languages were peripheral, while in the Blyden-Hayford model, they were central.

Periphery or the center—that was the great divide in the visions for higher education. The disagreement is still relevant as Africa struggles for a more equitable place in the global community of the twenty-first century.

In most of my publications, principally in *Decolonizing the Mind*; *Penpoints, Gunpoints, and Dreams*; and *Something Torn and New*, I have argued that language occupies a significant position in the hierarchy of wealth, power, and values in any society. Let me summarize the argument.

Language is a product of a community in its economic, political, and cultural evolution in time and space. In their very negotiation with nature and with one another, humans give birth to a system of communication whose highest expression and development is the organized sound that we call language. But language is also the producer of a community, for it is language, after all, that enables humans to negotiate effectively their way into and out of nature and that makes our multifaceted evolution possible. It is in that very negotiation with nature that a community comes to know itself as a specific community different from others. By doing similar things in a similar natural environment within similar rules that govern what is extracted from nature, how it is extracted, and how it is shared out, a community develops knowledges, which are passed from generation to generation and which become the basis of its future actions and the stuff of its way of life.

Every community has a way of life: a way of what, how, and when it negotiates with nature, how its members negotiate with one another, with other communities, with self, and with the universe. Language carries the cultural universe of the community, and in that universe also resides the entire body of values held by that community. Every community of humans with a given particularity has notions of what is right and wrong, bad and good, ugly and beautiful—a system of civics, ethics, and aesthetics, the entirety of which, with associated feelings, emotions, and attitudes, forms the basis of their identity, or their being for themselves. In *Decolonizing the Mind*, I described language as the memory bank of a people.

In his *Science of Logic* and *Phenomenology of the Spirit*, as indeed in all his works, Hegel often talks of being and becoming, making the distinction between Being in itself and Being for itself, notions that Jean-Paul Sartre plays with in *Being and Nothingness*, further talking about Being for others. We can think of being *in* itself as when an entity exists objectively undifferentiated, as opposed to being *for* itself when it becomes aware of itself as an entity. Language is what most helps in the movement of a community from a state of being in itself to a state of being for itself, and this self-awareness is what gives the community its spiritual strength to keep on reproducing its being as it continually renews itself in culture, in its power relations, and in its negotiations with its entire environment. It is its culture that enables a community to imagine and reimagine itself in history.

Culture is to a community what a flower is to a plant. A flower is very beautiful, very colorful, often very delicate, but it often readily defines the identity of the plant. Most important, the flower yields the seeds that make reproduction of the roots and trunks of that plant possible. Kill the tree trunk and even the roots, but retain the seeds, and the tree can reproduce itself. It can, if you like, reimagine itself. Language, the carrier of culture, is the ultimate and primary means of individual and collective self-imagination.

Empire builders have always known that, and in shaping how the dominated imagined their future, they clearly saw the importance of delinking the elites of the dominated communities from their languages and literally transplanting their minds in the languages of the imperial centers. Wherever the traditional elite resisted the transplant, because they were rooted in their own languages and cultures, the empire builders simply manufactured a new elite through a massive cultural surgery and engineering carried out in the new schools and colleges. The aim, realized or not, was to turn the elite into beings belonging to the imperial others even in their conception of themselves.

The Horton-Asquith model had a whole colonial tradition and theory behind it. It was inherited almost unaltered in the era of independence. The products of this model, this Macaulayesque system of education, spread out to fill the vacant places of white colonial judges, prosecutors, defense lawyers, lawmakers, governors, military leaders, and heads of departments of education. What an inheritance for Africa! It was an interesting twist of historical fate that those nurtured in the colonial mold should hold the key in molding the new nations in the military, educational, and economic realms.

It is ironic and interesting to compare them with the elites who, before the Asquith colleges were set up in Africa, were educated in London, Paris, and Washington. They lit the fires of nationalism, Pan-Africanism, and the cultural-identity politics of negritude and African personality. Whether they routinely spoke African languages or not, they still paid homage to them. Julius Nyerere translated the works of Shakespeare into Kiswahili. Kwame Nkrumah set up the Bureau of African Languages. In Senegal, poet Birago Diop and historian Cheikh Diop both stressed the centrality of African languages in the self-emancipation of the continent. Nevertheless, the products of the Asquith colleges embraced the English language with an almost religious fervor as the language of modernization and respect in the global community. In various ways, they argued, and sought to convince themselves, that English was now an African language.

The result is a paradox. Systems of education entrusted by the new nations to research ideas for emancipating and modernizing Africa, systems in which the new nations invested a good percent of their GNP, now nurture brilliant intellects in every field of modern learning who can't put even a summary of what they have acquired in any African language.

There is no doubt that these colleges, particularly in their heydays, have produced remarkable work. African scholars whose first degrees were acquired in the colleges of the Horton-Asquith model are to be found in major universities in Africa and abroad. But they are clearly alienated intellects, exiles at home and abroad, in search of a place they can truly claim as their own.

In the context of the collective social body, they become beings for others, at the very least beings against themselves, against the very soil that gave birth to them. African-language communities pay for intellects who cannot put a single idea, even about agriculture or health or business, or democracy, or finance, into the very languages that gave them birth. This great paradox of African scholarship is best mirrored in the production of African literature.

Because English was central to all aspects of learning in the new colleges, the English departments were very prestigious. Frankly, it is difficult to quite express in words the tremendous prestige a good performance in English gave. Students of English were the elite of the elite, and a first-class degree in English was simply the first among equals. At the center of that curriculum was the history of English Literature, "from Spenser to Spender," in the phrase coined by Professor Abiola Irele and adopted by poet J.P. Clark-Bekederemo. Since all the new colleges were largely external affiliates of the University of London, they all offered virtually the same history of the same authors, whether one went to Makerere in Uganda or Ibadan in Nigeria. And that is why in the Ashby description of the rise of these universities I could see myself so clearly.

I was definitely a product of the Horton-Asquith model, as were indeed nearly all the pioneering writers of the fifties and sixties. We were products of the English departments, and often our initial inspirations were triggered by admiration or criticism of the models we read, a practice Clark-Bekederemo once explicated in a book as following *The Example of Shakespeare*.

A cursory glance at some of the early titles of African fiction tells the story. The titles of Chinua Achebe's *Things Fall Apart* and *No Longer at Ease* were taken from W.B. Yeats's "The Second Coming" and T.S. Eliot's "Journey of the Magi."

The title of my own first published novel, *Weep Not, Child*, was taken from Walt Whitman. And I am sure that within the narratives or the poetry it is possible to hear echoes of Thomas Hardy, Charles Dickens, D.H. Lawrence, Joseph Conrad, T.S. Eliot, and Ezra Pound.

Although English examples may have given titles or even models to the new novelists, the encounter with images of Africa in the English novels that they studied often made African writers want to create correctives.

In his essay "Named for Victoria, Queen of England," Achebe tells us that his initial motivation to write came from his encounter with some appalling novels about Africa, including Joyce Cary's *Mister Johnson*, and he decided "that the story we had to tell could not be told for us by anybody else no matter how gifted or well intentioned."

It is quite ironic that, while one of the biggest achievements of the Horton-Asquith model was the production of an African literature in English, it was a literature often motivated by Edward Blyden's vision of positive affirmation of the African image. Writing in 1883, Blyden had expressed horror at the images of Africa in the English canon, especially at the way their constant repetition erodes the sense of self, just as, in a famous line of Ovid, water wears away stone by "falling often":

> In all English-speaking countries, the mind of the intelligent Negro child revolts against the descriptions given in elementary books—geographies, travels, novels, histories—of the negro, but though he experiences an

> instinctive revulsion from the caricatures and misrepresentations, he is obliged to continue, as he grows in years, to study such pernicious teachings. After leaving school he finds the same things in newspapers in quasi-scientific works, and after a while—*saepe cadendo*—they begin to seem the proper things to say about his race, and he accepts what, at first, his unbiased feelings naturally and indignantly repelled. Such is the effect of repetition. . . . Having embraced, or at least assented to these errors and falsehoods about himself, he concludes that his only hope of rising in the scale of respectable manhood is to strive after whatever is most unlike himself and most alien to his taste.

The words and the sentiments are echoed in the twentieth century by one of the most prominent products of the new colleges.

In the famous 1963 essay "The Novelist as a Teacher," Achebe wrote, "If I were God, I would regard as the very worst our acceptance, for whatever reason, of racial inferiority." He went on to define his role as a writer as that of an educator trying to help "my society regain belief in itself and put away the complexes of the years of denigration and self-denigration."

Thus this literature had two contradictory tendencies. It was often motivated and driven by the nationalistic and racial pride inherent in assumptions of the Blyden model, and yet its models were often the English authors read in class. But though written in a European language, it has nevertheless become the nearest thing to a common Pan-African heritage.

When Wole Soyinka won the Nobel Prize for Literature, his achievement and recognition were celebrated in many parts of Africa—Kenya, for instance. Names of writers like Achebe, Ama Ata Aidoo, and Ayi Kwei Armah are known and respected in the four corners of the continent.

Because of the models of its inspiration—the nineteenth-century Victorian novel with its natural realism and linear narrative structure, for instance—the literature, and particularly its narratives, tends to be conservative, almost imitative in form, and yet very pertinent in their descriptions of the concerns of twentieth-century Africa. Even in form, the writing seems innovative, different from its models.

What gives it this innovative feel? It cannot be the models that inspired it, in either anger or pleasure. Surely its newness comes from its relationship to African languages and the great heritage of orature (oral literature) in those languages. These tongues are a reservoir of images, proverbs, riddles, and ballads, stories from which literature in European languages draws freely and often creatively. Among the Igbo (formerly Ibo), as Achebe wrote in *Things Fall Apart,* the proverb is like the palm wine with which words are eaten. In Achebe's case, those proverbs from which he draws so freely are a product of the Igbo language.

Native languages are the magic fountain from which African literature in English or French or Portuguese draws a perpetual youthfulness. The paleness arising from its imitation and the use of European languages to represent the real-life speech of the characters is immediately refreshed in color by the stamina and blood it draws from African languages.

All this—its Pan-African reach, its racial pride, its championing of human and democratic values—is the most positive side of what now I call Europhone African literature. Its Europhonity is, of course, a direct product of the Horton-Asquith model, and so whatever is postive in it would justify Horton's hope that the great achievements of the classics and Western civilization would generate excellence in the African recipients.

However, Europhonism has no language or a cultural universe of its own. The literature it generates—Europhone African literature—is given its identity in the marketplace of all writings in European tongues by all the reservoir of images in African life and languages. It has therefore a negative, almost parasitic side to it. Like a leech, it sucks blood and stamina from African languages, but it never gives anything back to the languages and the orature from which it draws so freely to give it that identity in the marketplace of worldwide writings in European tongues, global Europhone literature.

The two tendencies inherent in Europhone African literature are actually true of all the scholarship produced by the Horton-Asquith model. There is the creative tendency. The scholarship takes away from the African heritage and produces great works on many aspects of African history and landscape, most of which are now to be found in libraries all over the world. But there is also the parasitic aspect to this scholarship, which knows only how to take away but never how to give anything back to the languages and peoples on whose behalf it makes its claim in the global community of scholarship in the arts, sciences, and technology.

Knowledges of Africa, the results of extensive research, invention, and discoveries about Africa by the sons and daughters of the continent, are stored in European-language granaries.

We can now see the implications of the Horton-Asquith model. A people can be deprived of wealth and power, but one of the worst deprivations is depriving them of the means of perceiving and articulating their deprivation, and thereby of developing a vision and strategy and tactics for fighting it. We can, of course, blame it on colonialism, and I have done my share of blaming in many of my publications, but remember that we cannot accuse colonialism of failing to do what it was clearly not meant to do. Colonialism and colonial models were never meant to develop the colonies for the benefit of the colonized.

That is why I think it is time that African scholarship and universities begin to question the Horton-Asquith model and its legacy of colonial language policy and practice.

In the academies of the world today, one hears of scholars of African realities who do not know a word of the languages of the environments on which they are experts. Schools in Africa and abroad are peopled by experts—African or not, sympathetic to the African cause or not, progressive or not—who do not have to demonstrate any acquaintance with, let alone expertise in, any African language. They hold PhDs on matters to do with Africa without the requirement of an African language.

The result is the marginalization of African languages in the academy at home. European tongues rule Africa. The same holds true at the global level. The culture and thought of the twentieth-century global community is largely dominated by a handful of European languages. Even the United Nations and its agencies assume the centrality of European languages in international relations. Thus, African languages become invisible intellectually and politically, at home and abroad. They are forced into intellectual and political death.

In her book *From a Native Daughter*, Haunani-Kay Trask argues that replacement of indigenous languages by colonial ones results in the creation of dead languages. But what is dead or lost is not the language but the collective memory of the people who once spoke it and transmitted their mother tongues to succeeding generations.

Everywhere, European languages have come shouting the often-quoted words from the *Bhagavad Gita*:

I am become death
The shatterer of worlds

We think of death too narrowly, only in terms of physical disappearance. Death comes in many forms, and there is the equally devastating cultural death. We Africans already provide a good example of such a possibility.

Over the last four hundred years, we have seen Africans in the West lose their names completely, so that our identity is seen in terms of Jameses, Johns, Joneses, and Janes. Now every achievement in sports, in academia, in the sciences, and in the arts goes to reinforce European naming systems and cultural personality. Language is, of course, the most basic of naming systems. With the loss of our languages will come the loss of our entire naming systems, and every historical intervention, no matter how revolutionary, will thence be within a European naming system, enhancing its capacities for ill or good. Thus every intellectual performance results in the enhancement of the cultural personality of white imperial Europe.

The question of language goes to the heart of the very being and existence of any community deprived of its language. That is why I now regard Europhonism as the most dangerous intellectual system. Its logic, for Africa, is the complete wiping out of the African personality from the global cultural map. We simply become one of several branches in the European language system, and the only struggle is for the recognition of the equal worth of all the cultural branches of a European global whole. Europhonism reinforces Eurocentrism.

African scholars must seriously take another look at the Blyden vision. The Blyden-Hayford model rejects the prevalent assumption about the relationship of Africa to the world, which equates knowledge, modernity, modernization, civilization, progress, and development to the acquisition of European tongues.

There are hundreds of languages in Africa and the world, each of which is a unique store of memories and thoughts and experiences of benefit to human life. It is true that the current revolutions in information technologies daily shrink the globe into Marshall McLuhan's global village. But they also open possibilities for expansion of the human community. Academic and other cultural institutions should be among the first to sensitize the world community to the existence of unfamiliar knowledge systems in the diverse languages of the world.

There are, of course, practical difficulties in implementing policies that realize the full plurality and diversity of languages, but there should be conscious efforts by various disciplines to recognize the existence of knowledge in languages other than those with origins in Europe and to find ways of tapping into the knowledges thus contained, and in the process help in the dialogue among languages. Dialogue among languages is definitely one way of giving back to any language from which we draw sustenance.

There are moves in that direction. In 1996 I attended a conference in Barcelona, Spain, organized in part by PEN International, which adopted the Universal Declaration of Linguistic Rights, based on the recognition of the need for equality and dialogue among languages large and small.

For Africa, though, the question of languages goes beyond that of simply sensitizing the world to the plurality of languages. It is at the very heart of our being and existence. And the main challenge is to African scholars and writers and universities to act as pathfinders.

It is this consciousness that made me turn to the Gĩkũyũ language for my creative endeavor. And I must say that my associations with unversities have helped in my resolve.

I started my novel *Mũrogi wa Kagogo* (*The Wizard of the Crow*), in English, while I was Professor of Comparative Literature and Performance Studies at New York University.[1] New York University also helped me found and launch

Mũtiiri, a literary journal in the Gĩkũyũ language, in which I published papers on every aspect of development, hoping that the journal would inspire more journals in African languages. The University of California–Irvine continued with the support for the journal.[2]

There was also the conference on literature and African languages in Asmara, Eritrea, at the beginning of the new millennium. It was supported by professors from various universities.[3] The conference brought together writers and scholars from every country in Africa who then wrote in African languages. The hope was that this would be the first of many to come to continue confronting the question of African languages, knowledge, and scholarship, and to raise the visibility of African languages and to celebrate the fact that despite all the odds against them African languages have refused to go away.

Ashby's book of his Godkin Lectures opens with two quotations. One is taken from a dispatch from the governor-general of India in 1934, in which he declared that the education to be imposed on India was that of the sciences, arts, philosophy, and literature of Europe—in short, European knowledge, a kind of Horton-Asquith model.

The other is from the 1959 charter of the University of Ghana. By then Ghana was independent, and the writers of the charter saw the university as taking its place among the foremost universities in the world. As a great seat of African learning, it would give leadership to African thought, scholarship, and development.

That lofty ideal is still shared by many African institutions and scholars. But the question of African languages is primary to that leadership in thought, scholarship, and development, and I hope that all the African scholars and writers will heed the call.

Let us go back to the magic fountain and draw that which gives power and knowledge to the real agents of social change in the continent—the ordinary man and woman who speak their language.

When African writers reject Europhonism as the only way of performing their being, they will bring about genuine revolution in their literature in content and form. Then we can draw from elsewhere, from whatever sources, to add to that drawn from the magic fountain, instead of always drawing from it and taking the water away to enrich other languages. We shall link with the globe without delinking from our own worlds.

Africa must use its languages and peoples as a strength with which it can leap into tomorrow. African scholars and writers and institutions must lead the way.

5

The Modern Patron: The Role of the University in a Global Community

When I accepted my position as Distinguished Professor of English and Comparative Literature and Director of the International Center for Writing and Translation at the University of California–Irvine, I was asked by some skeptics why I would leave my position as Erich Maria Remarque Professor of Languages and Professor of Comparative Literature and Performance Studies in New York to go to Orange County? Orange County, they said, would not suit my cosmopolitan character. New York University is, of course, a great institution, and New York is unique in its multicolored diversity.

I was attracted to move by the idea of the International Center for Writing and Translation (ICWT), but that was not how I answered my concerned questioners. My response was simple and always the same: "I am going to UCI, the center of the world." By that I meant no more than the fact that in a world like ours, every point on its surface is a center of the whole. The challenge is for the inhabitants of a specific point to see the links that bind them to all the other points. Every center should reflect the globe as much as the globe should reflect them. William Blake put it better when he challenged his readers to see a world in a grain of sand and a heaven in a wildflower.

This challenge applies to universities. The university, of course, has its traditional autonomy—what goes by the name of academic freedom, that is, a space free from the direct dictates of the state, a space free from the strictures of the nineteenth-century Prussian ruler who wanted the University of Jena to produce not learned men, but obedient subjects. In its autonomy, the university strives to teach its students and engage them with the best that has been written and thought in the world, to borrow the formulation from Matthew Arnold, and also, especially for a research university, to add to the best that has been thought and written in the world. We add our bit to the tradition of excellence. This involves asking questions that may never have been asked, climbing heights that have never been climbed, dreaming that which has not been dreamed, daring our minds to soar, unfettered. But universities do not exist in a vacuum; they exist in society. In that sense, they are part of the community, the region, the nation, the world. Their pursuit of excellence is in the service of the community and the world in which we live. In their composition of academic staff, student body, and choice of subjects, universities should reflect, as well as help, the social milieu of which they are an integral part.

This is especially important in a rapidly globalized world. Globalization has resulted in a world that is economically and culturally polarized. Despite the enormous growth in the means and capacity to produce real wealth and eliminate global poverty, we are witnessing a globe divided into a few *have-all* nations, mostly Western, and a majority of *have-not* nations, mostly located in Asia, Africa, and the rest of the non-Western world. Despite the fact that the location of natural resources is largely in Asia, Africa, and Latin America, poverty resides there, the trio of continents sometimes labeled the Global South. Moreover, the gap between the two groups of nations is increasing. And within each nation, even the wealthiest, the gap between the have-not majority and the have-all minority widens and deepens daily. The figure of the beggar and the homeless haunts every street of even the wealthiest of nations. The prison population is the fastest-growing demographic. When any nation has thousands of homeless people—shelter alongside food and clothing being the most basic of human rights—and millions of its citizens in prison, it surely cannot see this situation as a measure of great progress. The gaps of wealth and poverty, both between and within nations, are a basis of great national, regional, and global instability. These rifts exacerbate the confrontations of cultural fundamentalism, reflected in Christian, Hindu, and Islamic fundamentalism, for instance. Fundamentalisms of intolerance exist within and without every nation. The notion that my god is more of a god than your god can only further widen and deepen the gap between peoples and fuel the social volcano on which the globe sits.

In such a world, the university has a great role to play. Just as the university hosts different disciplines, which, while pursuing their particularity, should be in dialogue with one another, the university should be the modern patron of an intellectual discourse among languages and cultures. No university should be proud of monoculturalism or monolingualism. Building bridges between even apparently irreconcilable viewpoints is an important function of the university. Just as ecological diversity is important for healthy plant and animal growth, cultural diversity is important for a healthy and robust social life. In fact, cultural diversity is not an addendum to the intellectual life of a university; it is an essential. I believe it was Plato's most famous pupil, Aristotle, one of the earliest academicians of ancient Greece, who once wrote that while each one of us can know only a part of the truth, the union of many can illuminate a greater area of truth. An approximation of truth, of course, never the final truth. Given its very intellectual constitution and mission of truth and excellence, the university should strive for the aesthetic of a multicolored garden.

The pursuit of truth has never been without a price, and we only have to recall the fate of Socrates, the ultimate asker of uncomfortable questions, to remind ourselves of the occupational hazards inherent in the search for truth. Aristotle himself once fled from Athens, saying that he would not let Athens offend twice against philosophy. The history of ideas in the world is littered with the corpses of martyrs for truth. Nevertheless, the university must continue being the modern patron of those who ask questions that may disturb scientific, cultural, and intellectual orthodoxy. It must be a frontier that is at the same time a crossroads of cultures and thought. But we should take courage in the knowledge that crossroads of cultures were always the centers of civilization, precisely because it was there that the culturally comfortable were likely to see themselves in the light of another culture. Contact was always the basis of self-renewal.

At the ICWT, where we have developed programs and seminars based on a vision of the interpenetration of here and there, the *here* being contained in the *there* and vice versa, we have brought to the campus Native American, African American, Hawaiian, Samoan, Fijian, Maori, African, Indian, Irish, and Korean intellectuals. We have supported translators working in Martiniquan French, Indonesian, Hawaiian, Icelandic, Telugu, Tibetan Chinese, Gĩkũyũ, Kimbundu, and Xhosa. We have supported the translation of collections of Dalit literature, Iranian poetry in diaspora, and Sindhi partition literature. We take translation as conversation, for conversation assumes equality between those conversing. Otherwise, it would be a command, an order, or a prayer. In all, we envision a global conversation among languages and cultures inspired by the words of wisdom from Aimé Césaire, who once stressed the importance of placing different civilizations in contact, saying that "it was an excellent thing to blend different worlds; that whatever its own particular genius, a civilization that withdraws into itself atrophies; that for civilization, exchange is oxygen." The modern university should be the great refueling center for that oxygen. Perhaps Aimé Césaire put it even better in his great poem *Return to My Native Land*, where he wrote that:

> . . . it is not true that the work of man is finished,
> That man has nothing more to do in the world

But be a parasite in the world
That all we now need is to keep in step with the world
But the work of man is only just beginning
And it remains to man to conquer all the violence
embedded in the recesses of his passion
And no race possesses the monopoly of beauty, of intel-
ligence, of freedom
There is a place for all at the rendezvous of victory.

6
Makerere Dreams

Year after year in Makerere, beginning in 1961, we celebrated the realization of a dream that had been fought for in the streets of Dar, Nairobi, and Kampala for over sixty years. The Makerere Students Guild, with its tradition of free and fair elections on the basis of one person one vote, had already undermined the colonial practices and therefore anticipated this moment. What the guild had done for students would now be the norm for Tanzania, Uganda, and Kenya.

Tanzania and Uganda were the first to get their independence, but when finally Kenya came into the mix, we spilled into the streets of Kampala. In euphoria we allowed ourselves to imagine an imminent East African Federation. The imagined had been given credence by the physical proximity of Julius Nyerere, Jomo Kenyatta, and Milton Obote at an earlier joint rally in Kampala, at which we had danced and sung:

Tulimtuma Nyerere
Kwa Uhuru.

Kenya Uganda Tanganyika,
Sisi twasaidiana

We sent Nyerere
On a mission for Freedom.
Kenya Uganda Tanganyika,
We help one another.

We would insert the names of the other two leaders, Kenyatta and Obote, in turn. Why not? On the Hill, we had lived as East Africans, electing our leadership without regard to their regional origins.

Nyerere had once promised to delay the independence of Tanganyika to await the independence of the other two, if such a move would accelerate a federation. That did not happen. But now, with Kenya's independence after a ten-year bloody war, what was once in song seemed about to become reality.

For those of us on the Hill at the time, Wordsworth sums up the moment:

Bliss was it in that dawn to be alive,
But to be young was very heaven!

His words were in welcome to the French Revolution and the future it seemed to herald. Ours were in welcome to the East African Union and the future it heralded.

It was a great moment in our history as East Africans—a time when we dared to dream big, a time of magic transformations. Clearly, the magic rubbed off on me. I entered Makerere in July 1959, a colonial subject of a white-settler state, and left in 1964, a citizen of an independent Black republic. During the same period, Makerere changed from a colonial appendage of the University of London into an independent institution, the University of East Africa.

The University of East Africa, born on June 28, 1963, was formally dissolved on July 1, 1970, but I like to think of it as a transformation into three national universities, including the University of Nairobi and the University of Dar es Salaam, which in turn spawned more colleges and universities in East Africa. Whatever the changes in the quantity and even quality of these institutions, they shared certain continuities because of their roots in the Makerere intellectual tradition. Most of their faculty were Makerere graduates. But the one continuity that unites them most had origins in the University of East Africa: the degree certificates of the new dispensation would no longer draw their legitimacy from London.

To celebrate this historic moment of transformation of this great institution is also to commemorate a great achievement by every measure possible. Among its distinguished alumni, this institution boasts of presidents, prime ministers, doctors, agriculturists, professors, diplomats, writers, musicians, artists, and athletes from every region of Africa and the globe.

I have been to regions of the world I thought were off the beaten track only to bump into some Makerereans. I was reminded of this on my way to Nairobi from Southern California via London. I had just entered the business-class lounge of

British Airways at Heathrow Airport feeling a little worn-out as a result of a sleepless night across the Atlantic, when my eye caught an African person about to take his fruit salad. We nodded to each other, started talking. His name was Dr. Jones Kyazze, former UNESCO representative to the United Nations and then a member of the Muteesa I Royal University Council. He was returning from a Rotary International Convention in Lisbon and so, like me, was in transit. He had joined Makerere two years after I left, and like me, he was a resident of Northcort Hall. But unlike me, whose degree certificate still said University of London, his was fully from the University of East Africa.

This global spread of Makerere students used to be well recorded in the Makerere newsletter that Margaret MacPherson maintained for years. Her passing was the loss of a Makerere personality, an editor and a registrar of a scholarship that has made and continues to make a significant mark in Africa and the world. It is scholarship born of a century of dreams that has been Makerere since its foundation in 1922.

Makerere was the site of political dreams. Because it brought into one campus students from Uganda, Kenya, Tanzania, Zambia, Malawi, and even Zimbabwe, it was the perfect place from which to launch our dreams—not only of an East African Union, but also of a politically and economically united Africa that seeks its economic, political, cultural, and psychological legitimacy within its own being, not as an appendage of the West.

Makerere was also the site of literary dreams. The Kenya I came from in 1959 was under a state of emergency with the dead and the tortured often lying in the streets. We lived under what Frantz Fanon calls a nervous condition of the colonized in a white-settler town, a graveyard of many dreams. Makerere opened the space of my imagination. It was here, on the Hill, that I wrote my first two novels, *Weep Not, Child* and *The River Between*, and numerous short stories. My play *The Black Hermit* was written for the specific purpose of celebrating Uganda's independence. Makerere made the writer in me.

I was not alone. I was part of a group that included John Nagenda, Peter Nazareth, Jonathan Kariara, Bahadur Tejani, David Rubadiri, and Mĩcere Mũgo, to mention a few, who wrote stories and poems and essays for the English Department's magazine, *Penpoint*. Nearly all the East African writers of my generation were products of Makerere.

In addition to spawning East African writers, this Hill hosted the historic gathering of African writers of English in June 1962. Chinua Achebe, Wole Soyinka, J.P. Clark, and Christopher Okigbo came from Nigeria; Lewis Nkosi, Es'kia Mphahlele, Arthur Maimane, and Bloke Modisane from South Africa. John Nagenda, Jonathan Kariara, Rajat Neogy, and I represented East Africa. Also in attendance were Langston Hughes from the United States and Arthur Drayton from the Caribbean, giving the gathering a truly Pan-African dimension. There had been great gatherings of Black writers before, but they never met in Africa: Rome in 1956 and Paris in 1959. Makerere's was the first-ever gathering of Black writers of that scale in Africa.

These writers would later give us the nearest thing to a genuine Pan-African intellectual forum: the book, that is, African literature. When Achebe passed, he was mourned all over the continent. His novel *Things Fall Apart*—the text most discussed at the conference alongside the writing of Dennis Brutus of South Africa—is read throughout Africa. The works of others, like Okot p'Bitek and Wole Soyinka, and of later generations, including Tsitsi Dangarembga, Ngozi Adichie, and Doreen Baingana, are equally well received as belonging to all Africa. Makerere was the site and symbol of an East African intellectual community, but it also marked the birth of literary Pan-Africanism.

It was at this conference that the questions of who we are as Africans, nationals, continentals, or even diasporics were raised. It so happened that every single participant there wrote in English; the product of our imagination derived its legitimacy from London. The physical empire may have come to an end, but the very success of that conference marked the triumph of the metaphysical empire.

The colonizers' language is at the heart of their metaphysical empire, for language is the vehicle through which the mind voices thought. This is not just creative writing and literature. By its choice of language, the scholarship that has emerged since our formal declaration of academic independence from London has continued to be an integral part of the European metaphysical empire.

More than half a century later, it behooves us, the inheritors and custodians of that scholarship, to look at the implications of that continued appendage to the empire of European sounds.

I have argued elsewhere that scholarship, any scholarship,

is not a neutral activity, even in its conceptual vocabulary. No matter in whose hands, scholarship affects how people view social reality, including history and culture. For centuries, cartographers conditioned people to think that Africa is smaller than Europe. Some, in the West, often talk of the continent as a country.

Scholarship started and helped perpetuate the notion that Africa north of the Sahara, including Egypt, was European, and the south was Africa proper, with its horde of tribes in perpetual warfare. Some of these attitudes have changed, in large part because of enlightened scholarship, but still the nomenclature of north and south of the Sahara and the vocabulary of warring tribes have become enshrined in scholarship and popular parlance.

The other day I received an email from one of my progressive colleagues at the University of California–Irvine suggesting that we revive and rehabilitate the word and concept of *tribe*. He, and some other scholars interested in Africa and Middle Eastern studies, had been chatting on how to reintegrate the subject of tribes into contemporary historical, sociological, and anthropological research and teaching on the Middle East, North Africa, and Africa. While the email acknowledged that the concept of tribes had a very problematic history for anyone studying the Global South and the formerly colonized word, it stated that it was clear that the tribe as a socioeconomic and political concept and marker of identity was still quite relevant in many if not most societies we study.

The five-letter word, again! There was absolutely no negative intent in the suggestion. Still, my eyes popped. I had a few years earlier given a lecture at the University of Hawaii on the myth of tribe in African politics. I looked at how the five-letter word had been used by scholars and journalists to editorialize how people looked at Africa. It was colonialism that first created the template of X-tribe versus Y-tribe as a way of justifying conquest and control, or what Chinua Achebe's district commissioner in the novel *Things Fall Apart* famously described as the pacification of the primitive tribes of Lower Niger. Journalists use the template of X-tribe versus Y-tribe to explain any crisis in any part of Africa. They look at the communities from which the protagonists come, and everything becomes clear. It's the traditional enmity between X and Y; it's tribal warfare. Even respectable scholars often use the same template, only theirs is covered with copious footnotes and references to Aristotle and Hobbes.

The continued evaluation of events in Africa through the prism of tribes distorts the real issues driving African realities. Why are a quarter million Icelanders a nation and 10 million Ibos a tribe? Why are 4 million Danes a nation and 20 million Yorubas a tribe? Even when scholars and journalists don't use the word *nation* in reference to European peoples, they at least refer to them by the names they call themselves. They talk about the English, the Germans, the French, the Chinese. But when it comes to Africa, the word *tribe* must be appended. Hence the Yoruba tribe, the Zulu tribe. Ibo tribesmen, Gĩkũyũ tribesmen. An English person who gets a Nobel Prize in chemistry is rightfully referred to as So-and-so, an English person. An African who gets a Nobel Prize in chemistry is editorialized as So-and-so, an X or Y tribe person. In other continents, heads of government are referred to as presidents and prime ministers of their specific countries. African heads of state must be editorialized as president and an X or Y tribe person. Novelist Ngugi, a Gĩkũyũ tribesman, was imprisoned by Jomo Kenyatta, his fellow tribesman.

A recent Reuters article even talked about tribal blood. What color is tribal blood or bloodshed? The word is so tainted by its colonial usage that whatever cognitive scientific meaning it might once have had has been subsumed under its pejorative colonial umbrella.

The word *tribe* has become a code. Once the readers see it, they assume that the actors are doing whatever they're doing because of an inherent tribal mark on their character. In the process, the real issues of governance, democracy, property ownership, economic control, regional development, and corruption get lost. It's as if a particular person were corrupt simply by being part of a certain gene pool, supposedly corresponding to a certain tribe.

So my reaction to the email was quick and direct. Far from trying to rehabilitate the word and the concept, we should struggle against its usage. I want to emphasize that the scholar's call was honest. He said that he had been to the Middle East and North Africa and found the term in use. In other words, people in Africa used the term. My first reaction was that even when people in Africa use it, it's simply because they have internalized a negativity. The abnormal has become normalized into a normality without losing its abnormality. But my colleague's citation of *qabila*, the Arabic word for "tribe," started me thinking.

The Arabic *qabila* becomes *kabila* in Kiswahili and *kabira* in Gĩkũyũ. But even when those terms refer to the same grouping as referred to by the English term, they have a different ring and nuance to them. They are more descriptive of a fact than than they are a framing of difference in development and modernity. In my own language, the word *ruriri* has no negativity, being a reference to a community of people with a common language, land, and culture. The negativity in the terms *tribe* and *tribesmen* lies in the European languages, English in particular. The English word *tribe* in its colonial colors is the term of an outsider.

This vocabulary permeating European studies of Africa to this day was invented by colonial anthropology, which saw itself as the study of the insider by the outsider for the consumption of the outsider. Colonial anthropologists gathered information and put it in their own languages, and we cannot blame them for that.

What we can question is the fact that our various fields of knowledge of Africa are rooted in the entire colonial tradition of the outsider looking in, gathering and coding knowledge with the help of native informants and then storing the final product in a European language for consumption by those who have access to it. In other words, we still collect intellectual items and put them in European-language museums and archives, and people have to dig into those languages in order to access knowledge about themselves. Our knowledge of Africa is largely filtered through European languages and their vocabularies. Is it not time that our scholarship stopped finding legitimacy in European languages in the same way that Makerere, as an institution, stopped deriving its legitimacy from London?

When the Makerere School of Fine Art was founded, it used to import clay from London. Good art had to come from European soil. It was only when artists like Elimo Njau, Sam Ntiro, and Gregory Maloba came onto the scene that they said, "Let the children paint. Let them sculpt. Let them use whatever material is around them, including banana leaves." Thus begun a kind of renaissance of contemporary East African art.

In the same way that Ugandan soil was thought incapable of making good art, there are those who will argue that African languages are incapable of handling complexities of social thought, that like their speakers, African languages are riddled with poverty. The irony is that English and French had to overcome similar claims of inadequacy as vehicles for philosophy and scientific thought against the once dominant Latin and Greek. But the commitment of their intellectuals and the states that used those languages changed that perception. African languages need a similar commitment from African intellectuals and states, bearing in mind that no language had a monopoly of cognitive vocabulary, that every language, as Cheikh Anta Diop once argued, could develop its terms for science and technology.

Cynics will respond by asserting that an African language cannot sustain written intellectual production. How is it that 4 million Danes can have libraries and bookshops stocked with books in their language and 10 million Ibos cannot? Icelanders, who number about two hundred fifty thousand, have one of the most flourishing intellectual productions in Europe. What a quarter of a million people can do, surely 10 million people can also do. Today we talk of the Greek and Latin intellectual heritage but forget that these productions developed among regional cities connected by trade. The vaunted Italian Renaissance and its rich and varied output in the arts, architecture, and learning were largely from Rome, Florence, Mantua, Venice, and Genoa. The intellectual production that the vernaculars of these city-states, principalities, and regions achieved can be matched by any other similarly situated languages.

The question remains: What should be the place of European languages in African scholarship? No matter how we may think of the historical process by which they came to occupy the place they now occupy in our lives, it is a fact that European languages—principally English, French, and Portuguese—carry immense deposits of some of the best in literary and general African thought. They are granaries of African intellectual production. These languages have enabled a visible African presence in contemporary global culture. These languages enable conversation in a gathering of people from different regions and language groups. But it is only because we all had to learn these languages that we have to use them. There is nothing inherently global and universal about them. They just happen to be the languages of power.

Therefore the concept of enabling best defines the mission we should assign to French and English. Let us use them to enable dialogue among African languages and enhance the visibility of African languages in the world community instead of letting them be a tool of disabling by uprooting intellectuals and their production from their original language base. Use English and French to enable and not to disable.

As African scholars, we cannot afford to be intellectual outsiders in our own land. We must reconnect with the buried alluvium of African memory and use it as a base for further engagement with the world. African intellectuals must do for their languages and cultures what all other intellectuals in history have done for theirs. This then is the challenge to our scholars today: How best to connect with the African continent in the era of globalization? By writing in their own languages, yes, but dialogue among African languages through translations is also vital.

Such interplay can only result in the empowerment of African languages and cultures generally, making them pillars of a more self-confident Africa, ready to engage in a more equal give-and-take with the world.

If you know all the languages of the world except your mother tongue, you are enslaved. On the other hand, if you know your own language and add all the other languages of the world to it, you are empowered. Our choice is between intellectual enslavement and intellectual empowerment, and of course, I hope we choose the path of empowerment.

The scholar, however, cannot do this alone. He or she needs a publisher. Everybody knows how frustrating it is to write a manuscript and then have to put it on a shelf for lack of a publisher who is even willing to look at it. But the scholar and the publisher cannot do it alone. They need enlightened government language policies. Unfortunately, even African governments are buying into the recipe for African intellectual suicide. I don't know how much the monetary forces of globalization have to do with it, but African governments are turning their backs on African languages. They deny them resources, starving them to death where they don't strangle them outright. This is a far cry from the ways of Kwame Nkrumah, who on assuming power in Ghana in 1957 set up the Bureau for African Languages. Or of Julius Nyerere, who did so much for Kiswahili in terms of policy and also translated Shakespeare into Kiswahili. He was wrong in his attitude toward other African languages, but still, he did give Kiswahili the necessary power base. Nyerere of Makerere was also the first and only chancellor of the University of East Africa. Thus two of the most consistent proponents of African unity, Osagyefo (Redeemer) Nkrumah and Mwalimu (Teacher) Nyerere, were also the leading advocates of positive policies regarding African languages. I wish each and every African country would emulate the idea of setting up a Central Bureau of African Languages that would oversee the development and relationships of African languages in their own country.

In the particular case of East Africa, I would like to see three language policies: strengthen the foundation of its mother tongue, add Kiswahili as the common language, and then maintain the storehouse of English. In terms of books, I would love to see more translations among those three languages and of course among African languages as a whole.

Let the new generation of scholars extend the dream that was always Makerere and venture forth to open new frontiers of knowledge. Let Africa open new spaces in its economy, technology, sciences, arts, and culture. Let Africa be at the forefront in the renaissance of a new, more inclusive humanity. Let ourselves be the beginning of the new selves. Then will our dreams merge with those of millions of working people in our countries.

Part Two

Voices of Prophecy

7
Abdilatif Abdalla and the Voice of Prophecy

Though Abdalla and I come from two different regions of Kenya, he from the Coast and I from the Highlands, and we are different ages, he born in 1946 and I in 1938, our two lives are interwoven with Kenya's postcolonial history, and our paths have crossed at key moments of that history. I published my first novel, *Weep Not, Child*, in 1964 at the age of twenty-six; he published his first epic, *Utenzi wa Maisha ya Adamu na Hawaa* (Epic of the Life of Adam and Eve), in 1971 at the age of twenty-five. In *Kenya: Twendapi?* (*Kenya: Where Are We Going?*), the leaflet that Abdalla published clandestinely in 1969, he questioned the direction our country was taking, decrying the denial of democratic space and warning against an encroaching dictatorship. Though very strong on the question of democracy, the pamphlet had the shortcoming of seeing the emerging dictatorship in ethnic terms, denouncing "*wajumbe ambao wamewekwa ili kulifanyia kazi kabila Fulani ili lizidi kudhulumu makabila mengine*"—"leaders who have been forced on us to serve one tribe so it can continue to oppress the other tribes." In the preface to my third novel, *A Grain of Wheat*, published in 1967, I had warned against similar anti-people trends, but in class terms. I lamented the fact that the reality of the postcolonial situation was painful, sometimes too painful for the farm laborers and workers who fought against the British and who now saw all that they had fought for being put to one side. Despite our difference on the interests the new dispensation was serving, essentially both of us were warning against the consequences of the direction taken by the state only a few years into our independence.

Abdalla had written his warning after the banning of the Kenyan People's Union (KPU), of which he was a member, and the subsequent near-silencing of its leadership, including Jaramogi Oginga Odinga and Bildad Kaggia. The banning of the party had been preceded by the disqualification, on technicalities, of all KPU candidates in the municipal and mini-general elections of 1968. The grounds for disqualification were the most whimsical: that all KPU candidates had filled in their papers improperly but all Kenya African National Union (KANU) candidates had filled in the same papers properly. It was a crude play on the minds of Kenyans—contempt, actually, openly laughing at the populace. They used a fabricated legal technicality to subvert the law. They became economical with the truth to subvert the truth about the economy. They paid lip service to the democratic process to subvert actual democracy. For pointing out this truth, that the state had subverted the letter and spirit of the law, Abdalla himself was accused and convicted of sedition and placed in a maximum-security prison in Kamĩtĩ in March 1969.

This was about the same month that I resigned from the University of Nairobi as a lecturer in English in protest against the banning of a prospective talk by Oginga Odinga at the invitation of the students. I was not a member of the KPU, but I felt equally strongly about the shrinking of democratic space, a shrinking now extended to an institution founded on the values of academic freedom, the right to read and hear clashing ideas. This led to my first exile, voluntary though it was, which led me to Makerere, Uganda, in 1969, on a writing fellowship, then to Northwestern University on a visiting professorship, and back to Kenya to head the Department of Literature in 1972, the year that Abdalla returned home from prison. He had been three years in prison; I, three in exile.

On his return, he published *Sauti ya Dhiki* (Voice of Agony) in 1972; on mine, I published the novel *Petals of Blood* in 1975. Both took a consistent class position in the analysis of Kenyan society. This approach was best captured in Abdalla's dramatic poem, *Mnazi: Vuta N'kuvute* (Coconut Tree: Pull and I Pull You), in his depiction of the struggle between Badi and Alii for the fruit of the collective inheritance: *Mnazi ni wa shirika* (Mnazi belongs to the organization). In conceiving the poem, Abdalla may have had Kenyatta and Odinga in mind, but here Badi and Alii become representatives of the social forces of class, not biological ethnic entities. Badi and Alii are like Kĩgũnda and Kĩoi in the play, *Ngaahika Ndeenda*,[1] performed at Kamĩrĩthũ in 1977, which continued the class themes of *Petals of Blood*. The publications of *Petals of Blood* and *Sauti ya Dhiki* had two opposite though ironic results: *Sauti ya Dhiki* won the Kenyatta literary prize; my novel and the play won me Kenyatta's wrath and a place at the Kamĩtĩ Maximum Security Prison. I was thus the second writer to be so imprisoned in postcolonial Kenya.

As if to make the point clear, I was placed in a prison block near the one where Abdalla had been held for three years. Some of the prisoners would point to the cell where he wrote *Sauti ya Dhiki*. I wrote down my prison notes, literally drawing from the same prison air and environment he had breathed, and later, in interviews following the publication of my memoir *Detained: A Writer's Prison Diary*, in 1981, I was able to acknowledge Abdalla's pioneering role in postcolonial prison literature. It's ironic that—with all these parallels and close encounters, including sharing friends like Grant Kamenju, Walter Bgoya, and Ben Mkapa, and visting Dar es Salaam, where Abdalla worked in exile in the Swahili Institute before he moved to London to work for the BBC and later edit *Africa Events*—we had not met face to face.

Little did I know then that in the following year I would join him in London in forced exile from a Kenya that had moved from a de facto to a de jure one-party dictatorship, soon changing from a party into a personal dictatorship. It was during the post-1982 period that I came to know Abdalla and forged a political, literary, and personal friendship that continues to this day. If I may say so, the personal was sealed forever following my insistence that Abdalla be invited to a literary conference in Hamburg. It was there that he and Betgun Hage met, their hearts beat each to each, and years later the encounter of Betgun and Abdilatif gave birth to my friend Muyaka, whose name makes us go down memory lane to the great poet of classical Swahili literature.

Now, together in London, as writers in exile, Abdilatif and I and other members of the London Committee for the Release of Political Prisoners in Kenya, who included Wanjiru and Wanyiri Kihoro, Nish Muthoni, Yusuf Hassani, Shiraz Durrani, Neera Durrani, Wangũi wa Goro, and our Caribbean and international friends led by the late John La Rose, we would meet at least once a week for the next seven years to agitate for democracy and the release of all the political prisoners in Kenya. We rejected the legal fiction that the Kenyan state had used: convicting some in court as criminals, reserving the term "political detention" for those admittedly held without a trial. Under that fiction, Maina wa Kinyatti, many university students, and hundreds of others accused of links to the 1982 coup attempt would have been regarded as convicts, and those like Kamoji Wachiira, Edward Oyugi, Ali Al'amin Mazrui, and Willy Mutunga, held under similar conditions, as political detainees under the law. To us, they were all political prisoners because they had been taken in and punished for their opposition to the shrinking democratic space. Prison became a metaphor for the Kenya of the Daniel arap Moi dictatorship, echoing the lines by Muyaka bin Haji quoted by Abdilatif Abdalla in *Sauti ya Dhiki*: "*Ngome intuumiza / Naswi tu mumo ngomeni*"—"The walls torture us, yet we live inside them."

It was also during those struggles that I looked back to the pamphlet *Kenya: Twendapi?* and realized its prophetic character and import. In our different ways and with different details, we in the committee were really asking the same question over and over again, trying in the process to offer a vision that we thought provided the correct response. The committee, which was formed in July 1982 under the chairmanship of John La Rose, faced two enormous challenges: breaking the culture of silence and fear within Kenya, and changing the international culture of benevolent indifference to what was happening in Moi's Kenya.

In light of the democratic gains in the country today, it's difficult for people to quite imagine the fear that gripped Kenyan society, especially after the failed attempted air force coup of 1982. Mass terror followed the failed coup. Organizing in any way, shape, or form was criminalized. All persons deemed to be challenging the government or even simply defending the right to organize were hauled off to prison, forced into exile, or murdered. Because universities had always been centers of dissent, they became the objects of the state's wrath. Unsurprisingly, students and professors were among those targeted by the regime. Kamoji Wachiira, Ali Al'amin Mazrui, Edward Oyugi, Maina wa Kinyatti, and Willy Mutunga, to mention only a few, were among the victims. Thus pouncing on leaders of thought, those whose very raison d'être was to work in ideas, intensified the culture of silence and fear. The terror had affected even those abroad: all members of the London committee could tell stories of Kenyans abroad fleeing to avoid meeting them in the streets or corridors of universities. Although within Kenya people were organizing underground, it was also very important for them to know that Kenyans abroad were organizing aboveground and thus legitimizing the right to organize. We kept the idea of the right to organize in all the documents that we smuggled out of the country and published abroad. When later we formed UKENYA: United Movement for Democracy in Kenya as an aboveground organization, we provided a model for the others that later emerged in Kenya. Names like Forum for Democracy in Kenya clearly echoed our name.

At the same time, Kenya was deemed, in the West at least, to be an island of democracy and stability. Initially the committee had difficulties in puncturing that outlook, especially the more difficult formulation that Kenya was not as bad as, say, Uganda or Tanzania. I can remember the skepticism with which the Security Committee of the British House of Lords received our documented claims about the Wagalla massacre. Without the internet, we had to scour newspapers line by line to provide the data that was proof. Abdilatif in his strategic employment at the BBC had access to many newspapers and reports from news agencies. We also helped organize sister committees all over the world, in the United States, Sweden, Denmark, Norway, and Nigeria, which spearheaded campaigns of information in their own territories. The Swedish Solidarity Committee—founded by Eva Lanno and other Swedes but later joined by Kenyans, among them Gikang'a and Njeri—became one of the most productive, and its intense campaigning resulted in the cancellation of an intended state visit by Moi in 1987. We worked closely with other human rights committees for Chile and the Philippines, as well as Amnesty International. By linking with forces inside, we were also able to obtain details of torture in the underground chambers of the Nyayo House. One of us, Wanyiri Kihoro, returned to Kenya—against, I must say, our general warning—then was arrested and tortured in Nyayo House, but he managed to smuggle out, through his wife, Wanjiru Kihoro, the then unknown details of torture. We passed these on to Amnesty International, which then produced its special report on torture and human rights violations in Kenya in 1987, which finally turned the world around to our view.

The regime reacted to our activities by denouncing us as dissidents and traitors. In 1984, it had even sent its foreign minister Elijah Mwangale to Britain to plead with the British government to expel us from London. Within the country, the regime organized the public burning of our effigies and then threw them into the sea. There were even attempted assassinations, mine in particular thwarted by the Zimbabwe intelligence in Harare. To all their threats, we reacted in the words of Abdilatif Abdalla in the famous pamphlet: *Kitisho sicho kimfanyacho mtu kuacha lile aaminilio kuwa ni sawa . . . sisi twamini kitisho huzidi kumpa mtu ushujaa wa kuendelea na lile alifanyalo.* This was a position that the writer had also immortalized in his poems "N'shishiyelo ni Lilo" (This Is What I Hold Fast), "Siwati" (Conviction), and "N'sharudi" (I Am Back), all in *Sauti ya Dhiki*.

The poems serve to remind us of the obvious: that Abdilatif Abdalla is primarily a poet and not a politician; and that his real voice, the enduring voice, the voice that will survive him, is the one infused with the spirit of the words, rhythms, and imagery of his poetry, reminding us of the Keatsian words "Beauty is truth, truth beauty." At its best and most powerful, the aesthetic is also the ethical. The verses also serve to remind us of something else that is obvious: that Abdalla writes in Kiswahili, the national language, an African language.

Lest we forget, Abdalla is one of the greatest poets of the Kiswahili language, one of a long line that goes back to Fumo Liyongo, Muyaka bin Haji, and Shaaban Robert. He is also a central figure in the modern Swahili renaissance that has seen an explosion of novelists like Mohamed Said Ahmed of the detective tradition, Ben R. Mtobwa of the crimebuster-thriller tradition, and Ahmed Said Mohamed of the serious political novel tradition, as well as the rise of a completely new Swahili critical theory tradition, with such figures as Kimani Njogu. Translations mean that virtually all Europhone African writing is now available in Kiswahili, contributing to the spread of Kiswahili as a language with the vocabulary and syntax to cope with all aspects of modern science and technology.

The fact that he is a poet in an African language binds Abdalla and me closer. We may have traveled along different linguistic paths, but it is surprising, almost uncanny, how we have arrived at similar practices. I started writing and publishing in English, a non-African but official language. Today I write primarily in Gĩkũyũ but crisscross among three languages: English, Gĩkũyũ, and Kiswahili, through directly writing in them or through translations. Abdalla started writing primarily in Kiswahili, but now he also works in English. In fact, he edited *Africa Events*, an English-language magazine—but he has had his poems translated into Gĩkũyũ, thus also criss-crossing the three languages. This once led us to a moment I would like to share.

It was in 1994 that Abdilatif and I, along with other Kenyans, among them Karĩmi Nduthu, Kitur, Maina wa Kinyatti, Ngũgĩ wa Mĩriĩ, and Khamis Ramadhan, attended the Seventh Pan-African Congress held in Kampala, Uganda, at Makerere. Besides the participants in the formal proceedings, the conference had attracted small traders from as far away as Kenya. These ordinary men and women had set up a temporary open-air market at Makerere, hoping to sell their wares to the participants, who came from all over the world. Abdalla and I had not been in Kenya for many years, and the need to be in touch with the folk from home drove us to the new marketplace. The women, mostly Gĩkũyũ speakers, were excited to see the faces of these two dissidents. They knew me as a writer but didn't know Abdilatif as much. Afterward, I introduced him and offered to read them "Siwati" (Conviction), one of his poems written in prison, which begins:

Siwati nshishiyelo, siwati; kwani niwate?
Siwati ni lilo hilo, 'talishika kwa vyovyote
Siwati ni mimi nalo, hapano au popote
Hadi ni kaburini sote, mimi nalo tufukiwe.

I won't lose conviction, my values. Why should I?
I'll cling to my convictions, come what may.
I won't abandon conviction, here or anywhere,
Till in the same grave we buried together lie.

The women were in tears. The poem spoke to them directly in Gĩkũyũ about the situation in Kenya. Some, obviously forgetting that I had introduced him as a Swahili writer from the Coast, said loudly: So he knows Gĩkũyũ. I had to explain to them once again that he wrote in Kiswahili, that this was a Gĩkũyũ translation. They now knew him not only as a political dissident but also as a writer who voiced their concerns and anxieties. Their reaction left a big impression in my mind about the importance of writing in African languages to connect with the *mwenyenchi* (commonality), and equally important, translations as a way of making our languages dialogue with each other to the same end of reaching harmony—*wenyenchi.*

Abdalla's attitude to languages is thus another link that binds us. Though he is committed to Kiswahili, he has never talked of it as superior to other languages. He has respect for the others, which is why he has continued acquiring more. He has added Arabic and now German to his Kiswahili and English. He takes the equality of languages and cultures for granted. This is against the general trend. I have argued strongly against linguistic feudalism, wherein some languages see themselves as a kind of aristocracy in a relationship of power over other languages and cultures. Although the worst offenders are Western languages of the former empires, this arrogant tendency has sometimes arisen in many others. Linguistic feudalism should be replaced by the concept of network, in which languages and cultures large and small give and take without exploitation or oppression. Such a network assumes the equality of languages.

I believe that writers come from a prophetic tradition. A prophet looks at existing conditions and is able to deduce the future that is inevitable if current trends continue. He voices a warning. She points out, poses questions, challenges, and then calls for a change in the moral direction of a community. When people fail to heed the warnings and the consequences follow, they turn around (if they haven't murdered the prophet first) and ask: How did you know that this would happen? How could you have predicted this? I am sure that Abdalla has fielded those kinds of questions many times. But rarely in the history of prophecy has a prophet asked a question that lives on, continually posing new challenges to new generations. Abdalla managed to do this in his question: *Twendapi?* Where are we headed?

At a recent internet interview, Kimani wa Wanjiru asked Abdalla if the pamphlet was still relevant to Kenya and whether the issues raised therein had been adequately addressed more than forty years later. Abdilatif responded: "My very brief answer is that I would like to believe that the question is still very relevant, because I think as a nation, we have not yet sat down to seriously and thoroughly discuss what kind of country we would like Kenya to be, and also have the courage to take practical steps to bring about the structural changes needed."

So we continue to ask, *Kenya twendapi?* in our poetry, fiction, and essays. It's only in terms of the economy, politics, culture, and psychology, and hence our spiritual strivings for a new Kenya, that we can meaningfully address that question. Now as it did then, it calls for the economic, political, cultural, psychological, and spiritual empowerment of the ordinary man and woman of Kenya, of Africa and the world, irrespective of their gender, ethnicity, and religious affiliations. It is indeed a question that speaks to the globe today.

It is only right and proper, as we celebrate the life of a beloved poet, a political activist, a humanist, a teacher, an editor, a maker of dictionaries, a broadcaster, and a translator, that we ask: *Abdalla wendapi?* But we already know the answer. He may be retiring from marking essays and attending departmental meetings, but he will continue asking the questions that have always driven him and his voice of prophecy for the benefit of Kenya, Africa, and the world. Thank you, Abdilatif Abdalla!

8

Chinua Achebe: The Spirit Lives

I first met Chinua Achebe in 1961 at Makerere, Kampala. His novel *Things Fall Apart* had come out two years before. I was then a second-year student, the author of just one story, "Mugumo," published in *Penpoint*, the literary magazine of the English Department. At my request, he read the story and made some encouraging remarks. What I did not tell him was that I was in the middle of my first novel for a writing competition organized by the East African Literature Bureau, what would later be published as *The River Between.*

My next encounter was more dramatic, on my part, at least, and it would have a profound impact on my life and literary career. It was at the now famous 1962 Conference of Writers of English Expression. Chinua Achebe was one of a long line of other literary luminaries that included Wole Soyinka, J.P. Clark, the late Es'kia Mphahlele, Lewis Nkosi, and Bloke Modisane. The East African contingent consisted of Grace Ogot, Jonathan Kariara, John Nagenda, and me. My invitation was on the strength of my short stories published in *Penpoint* and in *Transition*. The novel most discussed at the conference as a model of literary restraint and excellence was *Things Fall Apart*.

What most attracted me, though, was not my being invited there as a "writer" but the fact that I would be able to show Achebe the manuscript of my second novel, what would later become *Weep Not, Child*. It was very generous of him to agree to look at it because, as I would learn later, he was working on his novel *Arrow of God*. Because of that and his involvement in the conference, he couldn't read the whole manuscript, but he read enough to give me some useful suggestions.

More important, he talked about the manuscript to his publisher, William Heinemann, represented at the conference by June Milne, who expressed an interest in the work. *Weep Not, Child* would later be published by William Heinemann and the paperback by Heinemann Education as the fourth in the now famous African Writers series, of which Achebe was the editorial adviser. *Weep Not, Child* would turn out to be the first new manuscript for the African Writers series, the numbers before it being reprints of previously published novels.

I was working with the *Nation* newspaper when *Weep Not, Child* came out. It was April 1964, and Kenya was proud to have its first modern novel in English by a Kenyan African. Or so I thought, for the novel was well reviewed in the Kenyan newspapers. The *Sunday Nation* even carried my interview by John de Villiers, one of its senior feature writers. I assumed that every educated Kenyan would have heard about the novel. I was woken to reality when I entered a club, the most frequented by the new African elite at the time, who all greeted me as the Kenyan author of *Things Fall Apart*.

Years later, at Achebe's seventieth birthday celebrations at Bard College, attended by Toni Morrison and Wole Soyinka, among others, I told this story of how Achebe's name had haunted my life. When Soyinka's turn to speak came, he said that I had taken the story from his mouth: he had been similarly mistaken for Chinua Achebe.

The fact is, Achebe became synonymous with the Heinemann African Writers Series and African writing as a whole. There is hardly any African writer of my generation who has not been mistaken for Chinua Achebe. Every African novel became *Things Fall Apart*, and every writer some sort of Chinua Achebe. Even a protestation to the contrary was not always successful. I have had a few such encounters inside and outside Kenya.

The last one was in 2010 at Jomo Kenyatta Airport. Mũkoma wa Ngũgĩ, the author of *Nairobi Heat*, and I had been invited for the Kwani Festival, whose theme was intergenerational dialogue. Mũkoma, my fourth son, and I fitted the bill perfectly. As he and I walked toward Immigration, a man came toward me. His hands were literally trembling as he identified himself as a professor of literature from Zambia.

"Excuse me, Mr. Achebe, somebody pointed you out to me. I have long wanted to meet you."

"No, I am not the one," I said, or words to that effect. "Here is Mr. Achebe," I added pointing at my son.

I thought Mũkoma's obvious youth would indicate that I was being facetious. But no, our professor grabbed Mũkoma's hands before Mũkoma could protest, grateful that he had at last shaken hands with his hero. The case of mistaken identity as late as 2010 shows how Achebe had become a mythical figure, and rightly so.

He was the single most important person in the development of modern African literature as writer, editor, and quite simply a human being.

As the general editor of the Heinemann African Writers Series, he had a hand in the emergence of many other writers and their publications. This meant a major investment in time, energy, commitment, and belief. He never bragged about it, even refusing the unofficial title of Father of African Literature. As a human being, he embodied wisdom that comes from a commitment to the middle way between extremes. And, of course, courage in the face of personal tragedy.

His novel *Things Fall Apart*, the most widely read novel in the history of African literature since its publication in 1958, became an inspiring model. It is his lasting legacy to African and world literature. At the launching of my memoir *Dreams in a Time of War*, in Nairobi in 2010, the guest of honor, P.L.O. Lumumba, a Kenyan orator, mesmerized the audience with his renowned eloquence, but even more so with the sheer quantity of proverbs and pithy sayings he included without notes, all of which came from *Things Fall Apart*.

Achebe bestrides generations and geographies. Every country in the continent claims him as their author. Some lines in his novels are quoted frequently as proverbs of universal wisdom. His passing marks the beginning of the end of an epoch, but his spirit lives on to continue inspiring yet more African writers and scholars of African literature the world over.

9
The Global Kenyan: A Tribute to Ali Mazrui

Ali Mazrui and I were not friends socially, and we did not always see eye to eye on politics and art. In his analysis of African politics, he emphasized ethnic conflicts, whereas I saw class conflicts as the prime mover. But our lives interacted in the most amazing of ways. In a documentary that Ndirangu Wachanga has made of the life of the late Ali Mazrui, he asked me what I thought of my fellow countryman. Mazrui, I said, is primarily a political scientist with a literary bent, and I, primarily a literary artist with a political bent. I knew he had this bent because, way back in the early sixties, as a guest editor of a special issue of *Ghala*, then the literary arm of the *East African Journal*, I had published one of his short stories. Later he would write the novel *The Trial of Christopher Okigbo*, which would confirm this bent.

Our first international conference together was the 1969 International Congress of Africanists in Dakar, Senegal, where, on the eve of the conference, President Sédar Senghor received us in his palace and, on shaking hands, told me proudly that he knew Jomo Kenyatta. The conference was attended by the leading Africanists of the time. When it was Ali Mazrui's turn to speak, a day later, the hall was packed, standing room only, with intellectuals from all over the world pushing and shoving each other for space. I had seen similar crowds at his lectures in Makerere, where he was the Professor of Political Science, the wunderkind newly crowned with a PhD from Oxford, towering over a campus that once rejected his application for admission. I had just resigned from the English Department of the University of Nairobi over issues of academic freedom, and it was Mazrui, together with David Cook, who came up with a rescue package that enabled me to teach creative writing in the English Department and a class on Pan-Africanism in the Political Science Department. It was from Makerere that Mazrui and I had jetted to Dakar for the Congress of Africanists, and it was on the way to Dakar that he came up with the possibility that both of us, a creative artist and a political scientist, might write a biography of Jomo Kenyatta. The plan would later be shot down by those around the State House in Nairobi, but the idea was intriguing. He was the first African professor of political science, and I would have been the first published African novelist to write about the first president of an independent Kenya.

I was in the dark when I had my first serious attack of asthma. I had no idea that I had this ailment, but one night, alone in my room at a hotel, I found myself unable to breathe. I remember crawling on all fours from my room down the stairs to seek help at the lobby. It was dawn. I hardly knew French, and the workers were equally deficient in English, but somehow I managed to scribble down Mazrui's name. It worked. They tracked him down to his hotel, and in no time, he was with me. I was now prostrate on the ground, fighting for every breath. Kenya had no mission in Dakar, so it was finally the British embassy, which represented Kenya's interests, that promptly managed to get me a doctor. It was magical: one moment I was dying for lack of air, and the next minute, I was breathing freely, normally. I was really grateful, but vaguely disappointed that we had sought the offices of our former colonizer for my rescue. The newly independent East African states in 1964 had sought help from the same quarters to quell the African military mutinies.

After my one-year stint as a Makerere Fellow in creative writing, Mazrui, through his good contacts with the late Gwendolen Carter of Northwestern University in the United States, enabled my invitation as visiting associate professor of English and African studies there from 1970 to 1971. It was there I began writing my third novel, *Petals of Blood*. It was this novel, together with the play *I Will Marry When I Want*, that would in 1978 have me sent to Kamĩtĩ Maximum Security Prison and later forced into exile. Somehow, Mazrui and I had earned the wrath of the Moi regime, I for work with the London-based Committee for the Release of Political Prisoners and he for his outspokenness on human rights abuses.

Years later, he and I would return to Dakar, Senegal, as special guests of the Council for the Development of Social Science Research in Africa for its thirtieth conference, where we were made life members. My honorary doctorate from Walter

Sisulu University in 2004 became special to me because Mazrui and Mandela received theirs on the same occasion. Two Kenyan intellectuals were honored at the same time, once by a prestigious research institution in West Africa and again by an African university in South Africa.

I'll leave it to political scientists to assess Mazrui's legacy, but for me, taking his intellectual output as a whole, he more than lived up to the image of the global African. He made Kenya and Africa visible in the highest echelons of intellectual production. To see him on the platform quoting from poets and philosophers in support of his arguments was to witness a master intellectual performer. He wined and dined and argued with kings, presidents, and generals, but he never lost his common touch. The attention and respect he gave to the voice of the student was the same as he gave to the mighty. He belonged to generations; they saw themselves in him.

I witnessed these qualities at close quarters at the conference of the New York African Studies Association in Binghamton in 2013 to celebrate Mazrui's eightieth birthday. Intellectuals of his generation and others who could as easily have been his grandchildren gathered and read papers in his honor. Among these "grandchildren" was my twenty-year-old daughter, Mũmbi wa Ngũgĩ, from Harriet L. Wilkes Honors College of Florida Atlantic University, who gave a paper on the politics of silence and agency. She opened her address by saying that there was no way she could have been left behind in celebrating a Kenyan legend and global African. Ali Mazrui sat through these celebrations, listening keenly to what the young had to say.

Mazrui was very fond of the Wordsworth poem *The Prelude*, welcoming the French Revolution, particularly the lines about the "very heaven" of being young during a historical awakening. I may not talk about heaven, but it was truly bliss to have witnessed Ali Mazrui's intellectual performance at the height of his powers. He shone, he dazzled, he enlightened. Some of that bliss can be found in his numerous publications, which will keep his spirit alive for generations to come.

10

Mazrui and Achebe: The Literary Artist and the Political Scientist

Until Chinua Achebe passed away, I did not realize the degree to which he and my family had interacted. When I Skyped my daughter in Florida that Achebe had passed on, Mũmbi closed her eyes and reminded me of their only encounter at Bard College during the celebrations of Achebe's birthday. She was then about six, and she drew a birthday cake on a piece of paper and presented it to him. Thiong'o, her younger brother by a year, remembers reacting very differently to the same Achebe event on account of my introducing him to Achebe's publisher James Currey. The five-year-old asked his mother for a piece of paper. He jotted down some marks, folded the piece of paper, and took it to James Currey. "Here, I have just written a book, will you please publish it?" James took the piece of paper, and of course promised to publish it. Thiong'o rushed back to our table, asked for another piece of paper, wrote another novel, and took it back to James Currey. James would publish that, too. Thiong'o returned with a third piece of paper. By the time he wrote his seventh novel, in just under ten minutes, surely a new entry for the *Guinness Book of World Records*, James Currey had resorted to avoiding the young writer. I think he left the party earlier than he intended. Being stalked by a five-year-old novelist was the price an Achebe publisher had to pay.

Ali Mazrui was not at the birthday celebrations, but there was a Mazrui there, his nephew Alamin Mazrui. Though I cannot relate similar dramatic family interactions with Mazrui, I have known the Mazruis longest, though in an abstract kind of way, because the Mazrui family history is synonymous with that of Kenya. I cannot think of another such prominent family, with an unbroken history all the way back to the encounter between East Africa and Europe in the sixteenth and seventeenth centuries. They have been active makers of the history of which I am a part. There has been a prominent Mazrui intervening in a crucial moment for each of the last four centuries. And yet I have never been mistaken even once for Mazrui, my countryman, the way I have been mistaken for Chinua Achebe, the West African. I can't use mistaken identity as a common point of departure in talking about the two.

Achebe and Mazrui were not intellectually or politically conjoined in the same way that Mazrui and Wole Soyinka were, first through their contribution to the Rajat Neogy–edited *Transition*, contributions that made the journal one of the liveliest intellectual fora for political scientists and artists alike, and second, through their famous polemics in the same journal. I stand to be corrected, but I am not aware of any polemics between Mazrui and Achebe.

What does a devout Muslim scholar, scion of an intellectual

and political family in East Africa, have in common with a devout Anglican, a second-generation African Christian family in West Africa? Both are steeped in the finest Western intellectual tradition, as likely to quote from Yeats and Wordsworth as from sages of indigenous religious and intellectual systems. Both are known for their measured responses to current events and their general adherence to the *via media*, the "middle way" between extremes. They shared the view of African contemporary culture as the triple heritage of the indigenous, the Muslim, and the Christian, or a variation of the three. On a closer look, we may find that they are branches from the same literary and political tree.

Ndirangu Wachanga, the maker of the Mazrui documentary *A Walking Triple Heritage*, once asked me to assess him in relation to me. I did not hesitate. Mazrui, I said, is a political scientist with a literary bent, and I, a literary artist with a political bent. The same contrast can apply equally to Mazrui and the late Achebe. Achebe has published many novels but also analytical texts with incredible political insight. He once wrote about bad governance and leadership in *Trouble with Nigeria*. And his last book, *There Was a Country*, is about Biafra. Biafra made Achebe turn to politics to understand it; Biafra made Mazrui turn to literature to understand it.

I regret that I once stifled what would have shaped up as an incredible debate between Mazrui and Achebe on Biafra. Achebe was a kind of roving ambassador for the Biafran cause, and in 1969, he came to Makerere to deliver a lecture, "Biafra and the African Writer," to which I was to respond. I was in Makerere on a one-year writing fellowship, following my resignation from the University of Nairobi in disagreement about the university's stance on the government's direct infringement on academic freedom. Achebe's delivery was measured, but it did not delve into the detailed politics of Biafra. It seemed to me that there was nothing to add to what came across, to me at least, as a personal testament. Mazrui came to the rescue. He was then the dashing young professor of political science, known to dazzle audiences with his incredible ability to yoke two or three apparently incompatible histories and somehow make them yield fire and light. Such was his famous description of Nkrumah as a Leninist czar or his linkage of Julius Nyerere and Milton Obote to Shakespeare and Milton. Mazrui asked Achebe several questions, and the debate became one between the two giants. Achebe ended his lecture with a reference to Albert Schweitzer, who spoke of the African as an elder brother while making the point that Biafra was fighting to get out from under the shadow of its Western brother. Mazrui ended up holding the Albert Schweitzer Professorship in the Humanities at Binghamton University, and in one of his lectures, he explained why he accepted it, later describing Albert Schweitzer as a benevolent racist, the conclusion Achebe had arrived at minus the benevolence.

Makerere and Biafra tie Mazrui and Achebe in a different way. The college was the site of the now famous 1962 African Writers of English Expression Conference. It was attended by virtually every African writer of the time, including Es'kia Mphahlele, Lewis Nkosi, and Bloke Modisane from South Africa, and John Nagenda, Jonathan

Kariara, and I represented East Africa. West Africa, Nigeria in particular, had the largest contingent, which included Wole Soyinka, Chinua Achebe, and Christopher Okigbo. The attendance of Langston Hughes and Jay Saunders Redding from the United States and Arthur Drayton from the Caribbean gave it a Pan-Africanist air. Achebe's *Things Fall Apart* was the model text against which other writings of the time were measured. But stealing the drama was the brilliant poet Christopher Okigbo, then working for the Cambridge University Press. Asked about the influence of T.S. Eliot, Ezra Pound, and Gerard Manley Hopkins, he retorted that he wrote his poetry for poets, a view he later reiterated and elaborated upon in an interview with Lewis Nkosi: "I am writing for other poets in the world to read and see whether they share in my experience."

Ali Mazrui was not at the conference. But when Christopher Okigbo, who had joined the Biafran war, died at the front, Mazrui wrote *The Trial of Christopher Okigbo*, in which he raised issues of literary and political commitment. Had Okigbo, the poet, betrayed the pen of a writer by taking up the sword of a soldier? By writing the novel, Mazrui had inserted himself right into the middle of the Biafran war. The creative invention was pure Mazruiana. Drawing on his triple heritage, Mazrui made Hamisi, a Muslim lawyer, defend Okigbo, a Christian but also in line for Yoruba priestly succession. In the trial, the triple heritage of Christian, Muslim, and African indigenous systems meet in a Western-style legal battle over a question that has been a central theme in the Western aesthetic debates over arts and politics. Okigbo, publisher, poet, and soldier, became linked to Mazrui forever in the Nigerian and, by extension, the African literary tradition.

Achebe was close to Okigbo, as were all the major Nigerian writers of the time. In a story in the March 25, 2013, issue of the *Daily Times*, the president of the Christopher Okigbo Poetry Society, Patrick Oguejiofor, was quoted as saying that, with the passing on of Achebe, the heavens will bubble because of his reunion with Okigbo. Achebe regarded his friend as the finest poet of his generation; he not only dedicated books to Okigbo but also wrote an elegy for the poet:

For whom are we searching?
For whom are we searching?
For Okigbo we are searching.

He described Okigbo as "owner of the riches in the dwelling place of the spirit," a phrase that could equally apply to the departed Achebe.

But Mazrui considers it an accolade that Okigbo is put on trial, charged with the offense of putting society before art in his scale of values. No artist had the right to carry his patriotism to the extent of destroying his creative potential. Mazrui saw the Biafran war being compressed into the single poetic tragedy of the death of Christopher Okigbo. The novel was published as part of the Heinemann African Writers Series, of which Achebe was the editorial adviser.

Through his position in the series, the Achebe of the Makerere event went on to nurture and inspire a whole generation of African writers. Moreover, his influence has been reborn in a new generation of Nigerian writers, notably in the work of Chimamanda Ngozie Adichie and Helon Habila.

Interestingly, in the works of these writers, in which the Biafran war takes center stage, Okigbo has been reborn among the group of Nigerian intellectuals in and around the University of Nigeria–Nsukka, who gather to argue and read poetry in Adichie's novel *Half of a Yellow Sun*, and among the soldiers in Habila's *Measuring Time*. In *Measuring Time*, Okigbo does appear. Uncle Haruna, when he returns from the front, talks of his friend Chris who traveled with him. This kind of afterlife of Christopher Okigbo is anticipated in Mazrui's novel.

While the storyteller launched new writers who dabble in politics and history, the political scientist launched the African literary tradition of the fictional afterlife of artists.

Mazrui has written short stories. I published one in *Ghala* magazine way back in the sixties, and I am sure he must have many more in store, and poems as well. Achebe has also published political pieces, as well as poetry in Igbo.

However, any discussion about them raises the larger question of the relationship between art and politics. Politics is about the organization and management of power in society. Art, literature in particular, is about the organization and management of values in society, the way power is organized, who or what social groups control it, the ends to which it is put, and its impact on the entire human realm, on the quality of human life. Ultimately, this is what the work of both

Achebe and Mazrui is all about. One iroko tree has fallen, but the other still stands strong among us.

The work of two of Africa's finest public intellectuals will always live, and it is only fitting that it is at Mazrui's event that we remember this son of Africa, who now dwells in AfterAfrica.

11

Wole Soyinka: The Conscience of Africa

Even before his arrival at the now famous 1962 Conference of Writers of English Expression held at Makerere University in Kampala, Uganda, Wole Soyinka's fame as a guitar-playing poet and playwright and member of the nascent Mbari Writers Club had preceded him through the accounts of Gerald Moore, one of the organizers of the conference. Moore was then director of the Extramural Department at Makerere and also a friend of Ulli Beier, with whom he would a year later put together the *Penguin Book of Modern African Poetry*. I don't recall a single text by Soyinka dominating the conference the way Achebe's *Things Fall Apart* did; nor do I remember his remarks sparking fire the way Okigbo's quip that he wrote his poetry for poets did. Nevertheless, he was a major presence at the conference.

Soyinka had already written and published a considerable body of work, including the plays *The Swamp Dwellers*, *A Dance of the Forests*, and *The Lion and the Jewel*. He had shown the literary versatility and output that later, in 1986, would earn him the Nobel Prize in Literature. But at the conference he was just a writer among other writers, whose sensibilities were shaped by their experience of colonialism, apartheid, and anticolonial nationalism. These writers were also united by a vision of the possibilities of a different future for Africa. Ever the realist, Soyinka had already punched holes in any starry-eyed vision of the future with *A Dance of the Forests*. Elsewhere, he had coined the cautionary line, "A tiger does not sing its tigritude; it pounces," in response to tendencies in some negritude poetry to typify the African past as glorious and conflict-free. Because of the stories preceding him, I expected him to stand up and recite "Telephone Conversation," the poem that Gerald Moore would always talk about, or play the guitar the way Moore had described it. He did neither. But I did see him once at Top Life nightclub, the most famous nightspot in Kampala at the time, dancing the cha-cha. Even some of the other dancing pairs paused to enjoy his moves.

I was then a second-year student of English at Makerere and the author of a few short stories published locally. To me, having never set foot beyond Kenya or Uganda, Soyinka's world of Ibadan, Leeds, and the Royal Court in London sounded far away. If we had never met again, I would still have carried the image of Soyinka on the dance floor, an image of the exuberant life that was Makerere and Kampala, a life of creative tolerance and acceptance of difference that a few years later would be shattered by the rise of Idi Amin.

However, our paths would cross again and again, at conferences mainly—in real locations in Africa, Europe, and the United States, but also in symbolic spaces of prison and exile.

Even at the time of the Makerere encounter, though without my knowing it, we had already met in history. In London in 1959, he took a stand on the Hola Massacre in Kenya, at which eleven members of the Mau Mau liberation movement were bludgeoned to death at a detention camp under the supervision of British officers. My cousin Gicini Ngũgĩ, one of the Mau Mau hardcores, as those who refused to cooperate were called, was in Hola at the time, and my brother was in a similar concentration camp in Manyani. In his Nobel Lecture years later, Wole Soyinka referred to the massacre—or the little matter of eleven men dead. But the little matter was a turning point. The whole world now knew. At the event at the Royal Court Theater, the empire was on trial. Thus, the writer at Makerere was already part of the Kenyan anticolonial struggle.

Our next encounter after Makerere was in 1967 at the Afro-Scandinavian writers conference held in Uppsala, Sweden, organized by Per Wästberg. Dan Jacobson, Wole Soyinka, and I were supposed to present our memories of childhood. For some reason, I could not find anything to say about my childhood, and I presented an excerpt from my novel *A Grain of Wheat*, in progress at the time. But Jacobson and Soyinka recounted their early experiences. What would later become Soyinka's nove *Aké* may well have been born at Uppsala. However, it was not Soyinka's memories of childhood that dominated the conference but rather the question of the gun and the pen in social struggle, triggered by the now well known 1964 incident in which Soyinka allegedly held a radio station at gunpoint to replace Ladoke Akintola's official victory address with Soyinka's own critical statement.

Soyinka's brief arrest was a forerunner of his eventual imprisonment for striving for peace in a conflict that would plunge Nigeria into a civil war over the Biafran secession, an experience that led to his prison memoir, *The Man Died*. The book came out in 1972, but little did I then know that *The Man Died* would visit me in Kamĩtĩ Maximum Security Prison five years later. I was put in Kamĩtĩ for my activities with the Kamĩrĩthũ Community Theater, principally because of my play *I Will Marry When I Want*, co-authored with Ngũgĩ wa Mĩriĩ. I joined a group of political prisoners already there, but we lived in solitary confinement, one man per cell. We were not allowed pen and paper and certainly no books except the Bible and the Quran. But suddenly one day a package of my books was allowed through. Any material that had the word *colonialism* had been censored. No works with politics in them were allowed through. Amazingly, Soyinka's *The Man Died* was among the religious and apparently innocuous texts allowed to reach me. I have always wondered whether they thought it a religious text or some kind of metaphysics of death. After all, my cell block was between the block for those condemned to die and the block for those thought to be deranged. Soyinka's *The Man Died* was read by every political prisoner as a testament of hope, not a treatise on death. I have narrated this in my own prison memoir, *Detained*. To this day I still find inspiring the line, "The man dies in he who keeps silent in the face of tyranny."

I came out of prison in December 1978, following the death of the authoritarian Big Man Jomo Kenyatta and the accession to power of dictator Big Man Daniel arap Moi. My daughter Njoki, born when I was in prison, was now among the family members who welcomed me home. In an act of solidarity, Soyinka had named her Ayerubo, a name she still carries to this day.

Can it get closer to home than that? We have met in other places, sharing the common experience of writers in exile. The most memorable time was in Leeds in 2007, when Soyinka robed me for my honorary doctorate, an honor he himself had received in 1972. The occasion reminded me that Leeds was our common alma mater. I went to Leeds in 1965, after Makerere, to find echoes of Soyinka, who had been there before me. The Leeds of my time had brought together students from all over the world. I still recall two students from Iraq who had been condemned to death in absentia by the Ba'athist leadership that took power in 1963 for their alleged membership in the banned Iraqi Communist Party. To me they were marked men, but they did not seem to be overly concerned. When, in 1994, I had read that Soyinka was condemned to death in absentia by the dictator Sani Abacha, I recalled the images of the two Iraqi students on the Leeds campus. As Soyinka was putting the ceremonial hood on me, the experience of the two students and his own merged in my mind.

There is also the irony of my current residence in Southern California. Our two roads from the Makerere of 1962 to different parts of the world had finally led us to the City of Angels. Soyinka, along with Jacques Derrida, was on the board of directors of the International Center for Writing and Translation of the University of California–Irvine, which lured me from New York University in 2002 to become Distinguished

Professor of English and Comparative Literature and run the center. Irvine is only half an hour away from Loyola Marymount University, where Soyinka was professor-in-residence.

We last shared a platform at Loyola Marymount in 2010. We both read from our memoirs, he from *Aké*, and I from *Dreams in a Time of War*. We had not planned it so, but we both read sections that dealt with our childhood experience of growing up during the Second World War. I could not help but recall the 1967 Afro-Scandinavian writers conference, where we were expected to deliver on memories of childhood.

To celebrate Wole Soyinka is to cerebrate the extraordinary journey of a remarkable man of letters, action, and conscience. He is a Byronic hero, or better, a Renaissance figure, dashing, defiant, and daring. His writings—the plays, poems, memoirs, and novels—carry one common banner: "the man dies in him who keeps silent in the face of tyranny." As a writer and public intellectual who has voiced his concerns over major happenings in the different parts of the continent over the last fifty years and more, he has become the moral and democratic conscience of Africa.

12

Mĩcere Mũgo: In Kenyan History, Literature, and Thought

Although Mĩcere Mũgo, née Mĩcere Gĩthae, and I were born in different parts of Kenya, she in Baricho, Kĩrĩnyaga, and I in Limuru, Kĩambu, our lives have crisscrossed and mirrored each other's in uncanny ways. For a start, we grew up in large families—in her case, her grandfather's, in mine, my father's. We went to similar boarding high schools, she to Alliance Girls, and I to Alliance Boys, both in Thogoto. The two schools literally faced each other across a valley. The students from one side of the valley referred to the dwellers of the opposite camp as Acrossians. So Mĩcere and I are Acrossians, she the younger by two years, but I have no memory of us having met as contemporaries at that time.

Meeting would happen in our post-Acrossian years, at Makerere, where I first enrolled in 1959, Mĩcere in 1963. I graduated from Makerere with a University of London degree in 1964, and Mĩcere Mũgo, with a University of East Africa degree in 1966—same classes, same departments, same college, same location, but two different certifications.

This was a reflection of the times in which Mĩcere and I lived. We were born subjects of the British Crown but graduated from college as citizens of the free republic of Kenya. The change of status of the college from an affiliate of London University to a constituent member of the University of East Africa marked the great transition in our countries from colony to independent state.

Mĩcere, more than any other Kenyan I know, came to embody the politics of that transition, carrying the twin burdens of hope and responsibility on her young shoulders. Her role in this transition, from colony to independence, will be better understood if seen in the context of Kenya's colonial history.

Unlike Nigeria, Ghana, and Uganda, which were protectorates, Kenya was a settler colony, like Algeria, Zimbabwe, and South Africa.[1] British settlers flowed into Kenya following the allocation of the country to the British sphere of influence after the Berlin Conference of 1884–85, especially after the construction of a railway line that opened the hinterland for white settlement and adventure. They renamed the Kenyan people's lands, calling them the White Highlands. The Kenya colonial state was a racial state, arbitrating a society in the shape of a pyramid, with whites at the top, Asians in the middle, and Africans at the bottom. Everything was run on racial lines: the very best public facilities were for Europeans only, the second best for Asians only, and the worst for Africans. The last were so bad that I do not need to say the words "Africans only." Education was run the same way: white schools were the best equipped in terms of buildings, land, staff, and books, and all these were paid for by our taxes. As the Mau Mau–led liberation struggle forced changes, it was clear by 1960, when Mĩcere was in her fourth year at Alliance Girls, that Kenya would regain its independence. There was a scramble to dismantle the apartheid structures, the most obvious being the previously segregated schools.

Mĩcere, the bright, beautiful, charismatic young Acrossian, was wrenched out of an African school to become a guinea pig in a previously Europeans-only secondary school, Limuru Girls, where she would live for two years. Her case has parallels in the United States to the Little Rock Nine, who enrolled in the Arkansas capital's formerly all-white Central High School in 1957, following the *Brown v. Board of Education* Supreme Court decision, which stated that separate educational facilities were inherently unequal. In Kenya, it was not a single decision by a court but the very specter of a new constitution that necessitated the scramble for desegregation. There were differences. Those in Arkansas needed troops to ensure their entry; Mĩcere did not need troops. The Little Rock students were nine; Mĩcere was the only one. The other person of color was the one Asian girl.

Having never been in such a situation, I can only imagine what it must have felt like to be the hope of a new nation in a hostile environment. Fortunately, we have her words for how it felt: "Being at the school was like facing a monster. I felt angry, upset, and alone." Mĩcere rose to the occasion and the demands of the time by excelling in everything, from sports, such as hockey, netball, tennis, and athletics, to debate and academics. She was in the school choir and was active in the drama and creative-writing clubs. She always performed at the top level. In her own words, "I told myself I had to be the best at everything I did." She had to do it all under scrutiny, for herself, her family, her nation, her race. It was almost as if she was there to prove our worth for independence. She was only one person, but for Kenyans, she was the One!

It must have been a relief for her to get to Makerere, where the majority on campus, in Kampala, and in Uganda as a whole, was clearly African and visibly Black. The Uganda she came to in 1963 was now one year old as an independent country. Even then her charisma and her intellect shone through. I remember her well because she and I were students in the English Department, and more important, we worked on *Penpoint*, the department's literary journal, of which I was editor. She took over a year or so as the first female editor of the magazine.

After Makerere, Mĩcere would go on to acquire other firsts. She was the first Kenyan woman deputy headmaster of Alliance. She was the first Kenyan, man or woman, to get a PhD in literature, which she did in 1973 at the University of New Brunswick, writing specifically on the different visions of Africa in the works of two African writers, Chinua Achebe and me, and Elspeth Huxley and Margaret Laurence. That academic feat would later inspire many more PhDs, particularly by women. I have personally met two female Kenyan PhD holders who have told me how crucial the academic achievements of Mĩcere were in their own conception of their abilities and ambitions. She was the first woman Dean of the Faculty of Arts at the University of Nairobi.

Mĩcere, had she so chosen, would have climbed to the very

top of Kenya's hierarchy of power, wining and dining with presidents, ministers, and diplomats. After all, she had already proved herself a leader, particularly in the school system, as headmistress of two nationally acclaimed secondary schools, and was now in a leading position in the university's corridors of power. But Mĩcere chose a different path, the people's path.

As Dr. Mũgo, Mĩcere joined the Literature Department at the University of Nairobi in 1973. By then, what was formerly the English Department had gone through a number of significant changes, following the call for the abolition of the English Department that Owuor Anyumba, Taban Lo Liyong, and I had issued in 1969. But the initial changes, besides the change of name from English to Literature, were still compromises. It was not until 1973, when I became the chair of the department, that the revolutionary changes we had called for were implemented. Though new in the department, Mĩcere participated fully and contributed immensely to the literary curriculum that put Africa at its center and integrated the African American, Caribbean, Latin American, Asian, and European literary traditions. The central position of Africa was what was really new in the educational revolution.

We wanted to extend the revolution and its principles to Kenyan schools. I remember the fights we had with the European bureaucrats at the head of English and drama studies in the Ministry of Education. This is where Mĩcere's experience, as someone with a postgraduate diploma in education from Makerere and as a former headmistress involved in school curriculum, came in. Most of us participating had no direct experience of examination structures, and we could never have been able to argue against the bureaucrats who claimed to be acting out of practicality and not dwelling in academic clouds. But Mĩcere had her feet in both worlds. She was what I call a practical visionary. The new structures were passed, and even adopted in the ministry as the literature syllabus in Kenyan schools.

But a political storm would come and sweep us off our feet, one of the early casualties being the abolition of the school syllabus by the Moi dictatorship that took over in 1978. It is difficult to convey the atmosphere of hysteria and hostility that surrounded the Department of Literature and the changes we championed on campus and in the school system. We were denounced in Parliament. Moi once held a press conference on his return from a state visit in India to condemn the removal of Shakespeare from the Kenyan school system and the addition in his stead of Caribbean and African American Marxists. A dictatorship is ruled through a culture of silence and fear, and the Moi dictatorship was no different.

In a way, the seeds of the dictatorship had been planted earlier in the regime of Jomo Kenyatta, the first president of the newly independent Kenya. He had been a valiant Pan-Africanist anticolonial leader, and had been imprisoned by the British for eight years. He had been falsely accused of managing the Mau Mau uprising, which had been led by Dedan Kĩmathi. Following the pattern of his friend and comrade in Pan-Africanism Kwame Nkrumah, who left prison to become prime minister of Ghana, Kenyatta also graduated from prison to presidency in 1963. But the new government started distancing itself from the ideals of the uprising. The ideal of people power was replaced by elite power. Imperialism was seen as an ally, not a foe. This attitude manifested itself in the gradual elimination of the Kenyan anti-imperialist heroes from official calendars and public pronouncements. The heroics and sacrifices of so many were reduced to the heroics and self-sacrifice of one person: the Leader.

The situation—and this was the case not just in Kenya but throughout postcolonial Africa—is that described by Frantz Fanon in *The Wretched of the Earth*, wherein the global vision that guided the anticolonial struggle gradually shrinks to the level of the continent, then the national territory, then down to the regional and ethnic level. The symbols of the nation left standing are the flag, the anthem, the nationalized colonial army and police force, and of course the Leader.

> Before independence, the leader generally embodies the aspirations of the people for independence, political liberty, and national dignity. But as soon as independence is declared, far from embodying in concrete form the needs of the people, the leader will reveal his inner purpose: to become the general president of that company of profiteers impatient for their return which constitutes the national bourgeoisie.[2]

It was with horror that Mĩcere and I and many others saw our history being buried before our eyes. Memories of Dedan Kĩmathi became inconvenient footnotes. Our actual history was being rewritten from colonial perspectives.

Talks on Vietnam helped clarify the situation. Vietnam had been under French colonial rule until the defeat of the French forces at Dien Bien Phu in 1954. Then U.S. rulers took over. It had also happened in Latin America. Fanon had, in fact, warned against Africa following the path of Latin America, where countries had disengaged from Europe only to come under the economic and political sway of their more powerful neighbor to the north. A country could transition from the colonial to the neocolonial. Neocolonialism is a system in which a country could sing a national anthem, raise a national flag, and still have its economy and politics and even culture controlled from the outside. Imperialism has a colonial and a neocolonial phase. The struggle for independence freed us from the colonial phase. We had independence but not necessarily national liberation and social revolution. We may not have put it in those exact terms, but they sum up the shared ideological perimeters that bound us and our talks.

Our eyes open, Mĩcere and I realized that we had to intervene with the only weapons we had: words. We wrote and produced the play *The Trial of Dedan Kĩmathi*, in 1977, trying to capture the aesthetic of resistance at the heart of modern Kenyan history. It was a major intervention in the writing of Kenyan history and even politics; it reversed the trend of official indifference, even denial. It was a glorious moment, and whenever Mĩcere and I have disagreed on political or organizational tactics, we would recall that moment, and all would be forgiven. As we wrote the play, we met almost every day before classes and quickly reviewed what was happening in the country as a whole. We would talk, argue, and get back to work. The highlight of the very successful run was the attendance of Kĩmathi's wife and her children. She was a joy to see, and her reaction made all our efforts worthwhile.

Ironically, the success of the play was the beginning of the state's suspicions about Mĩcere and me. The police harassed us, accusing us of interfering in European theater. In the four days that the play was performed to packed houses, the only days given to us, the police, armed in riot gear, carried out daily exercises at the Central Police Station next door.

In the actual production, Mĩcere played the role of the woman guerrilla fighter and organizer. Here, another side of Mĩcere's many talents came to the fore. In a different world and history, Mĩcere could easily have made it to Hollywood or at least paved the way for Lupita Nyong'o. I have never seen the character played better than by Mĩcere. Maybe, on the stage, she was remembering the women we had met in Nyeri, Kĩmathi's birthplace, where we had gone to do research on the Kĩmathi the locals knew. The women were virtually pleading with us not to let Kĩmathi die. Our literary Kĩmathi was based on those interviews. Years later, Mĩcere would join other female scholars in rescuing the women independence fighters from silence.

The published script of the play, under the same title, carried our joint introduction. It was a manifesto for a new, engaged theater, a liberation theater. My own work since, in theater, fiction, and theory, has been shaped by that manifesto more than any other single document. Others, too, have obviously drawn something from the manifesto and the play.

The Trial of Dedan Kĩmathi has been produced in many

parts of the world, including FESTAC 77 (the Second World Black and African Festival of Arts and Culture) in Nigeria. The most cherished memory, for us, was the knowledge that it was produced, underground, during the antiapartheid struggle in South Africa, and also in the forests and mountains of Zimbabwe during the anticolonial guerrilla war against the Rhodesian colonial state. It was performed where it truly belonged: in people-based struggles.

After our own production, we were often seen as a dangerous political pair. "Whenever I see you together," one person told us, "I smell trouble." But it was trouble for a good cause: expressing our aspirations for a Kenya and an Africa aware of itself as an equal player in the world. As it turned out, the person was right in smelling trouble, but it was trouble visited upon us by the state.

In 1977, I was sent to prison for my work in community theater. Mĩcere Mũgo was constantly harassed by the police, sometimes through her own family. And in the 1980s, the Moi dictatorship forced both of us into exile, she in Harare, Zimbabwe, and I in London, U.K. In our separate places and our different organizations, we continued exposing the atrocities of the regime, initially to skeptical Western governments who loved their dictator. Eventually our efforts, together with that of many others within and outside of Kenya, and with the solidarity of a broad mass of people in Africa and throughout the world, all the political prisoners were released and, in 2003, a kind of multiparty democracy was ushered in.

These struggles have taken a toll on our bodies and families.

More than any other person, Mĩcere has had her full share. She did not choose exile. We wanted to be part of the creation of a new Kenya. We aspired to show what Kenya, relying on its natural, human, and mental resources, could show the world.

If you ever expected to see Mĩcere bow down in sorrow or self-pity, then you don't know the girl who once had to shoulder the whole of Kenya as the only African person in an all-white school. Mĩcere Mũgo is a fighter. Where there is a fight for human rights, she is there. In Canada, as a student, she was part of the Angela Davis campaign, and whenever I have met Angela, she always has had a few kind words about Mĩcere. Unfortunately, she has also had to battle with cancer and the loss of her beloved daughter Njeri, but she still walks tall, still smiles, and still retains a great sense of humor.

In all these struggles, her pen and her imagination have been at work. A scholar, a poet, a playwright, an essayist, and above all a teacher, she is one of the most hardworking and dedicated persons that I have met. I can never tell where she got the time and energy to be a mother and friend in happiness and sorrow to her two daughters, Mũmbi and Njeri; to teach and be there for her students, earning awards for teaching excellence; to write her books; and to give public lectures, and have them published in journals and books.

Among the debates we had in the heyday of our fight for new ways of organizing literature in Africa was the one about the place of oral literature. The Ugandan scholar Pio Zirimu coined the term *orature*, rejecting the assumption of orality as a lesser partner of the written word. Unfortunately, Pio Zirimu has passed on, but the concept has intrigued many scholars, none more so than Mĩcere Mũgo. The concept permeates her work, as you can see in her collection of essays *Writing from the Heart of My Mind*. It permeates her poetry and her plays. Even the title of her collection of poetry *Daughter of My People, Sing!* pays homage to performance. It permeates her public lectures, where she incorporates the practice in her relationship to the audience and makes them participate. In fact she has developed what is now popularly known as the onion theory of orature, which you can find in her book *Orature and Human Rights*. It is not the teary part of the onion that she is talking about, but the many layers one has to peel before one reaches the core.

It has been an honor for me to call Mĩcere a friend, collaborator, and fellow activist. She has been an inspiration to generations. She is a pathfinder, and I am sure that, even in retirement, she will continue finding new paths to freedom and liberation. A dreamer of hope does not stop dreaming.

In his thesis on Ludwig Feuerbach, Marx talked of philosophers as merely explaining the world, whereas the point was to change it. In life, thought, and action, Mĩcere explains the world, but she never loses the point of wanting to change it.

One of my favorite poets is the Guyanese poet Martin Carter, who among other works, wrote the poem, "Looking at Your Hands." I can hear Mĩcere Mũgo saying:

No!
I will not still my voice!
I have
too much to claim—

if you see me
looking at books
or coming to your house
or walking in the sun
know that I look for fire!

I have learnt
from books dear friend
of men dreaming and living
and hungering in a room without a light
who could not die since death was far too poor
who did not sleep to dream, but dreamed to change
the world.

And so
if you see me
looking at your hands
listening when you speak
marching in your ranks
you must know
I do not sleep to dream, but dream to change
the world.

13

Grace Ogot: My Literary Sister, Kenya's Literary Star

Grace and I first met in 1957 as rivals in a debate between Maseno high school and Alliance. Maseno hosted us. I led the Alliance team in support of the motion: "If you want peace, prepare for war." My side was winning until there came a single intervention from the audience. It was a woman's voice from the back of the hall. Dressed in a nurse's uniform and speaking in a calm, clear voice in support of the opposition, she said that people reap what they sow. If you want war, prepare for war. If you want peace, prepare for peace. No amount of rebuttal on our part could dent the impression she had made with her commanding presence, her voice, her words.

Who was the woman in white from Maseno Hospital who had sealed our fate? Her name was Grace Akinyi. I would learn later that she was the fiancée of Alan Ogot, who was my maths teacher at Alliance, who by then was studying history at the University of Edinburgh. Later we heard that Grace had gone back to England, where in 1959 she became Grace

Akinyi Ogot, the name by which she is now known in Kenya, Africa, and the world.

Her Christian name, Grace, fitted her personality perfectly. With her mellifluous voice, she was always polite, but bold and daring, knocking at literary doors that others may have feared to touch. To the best of my knowledge, she was the first Kenyan to contribute stories to the BBC, joining a host of other contributors from the Caribbean and other places. such as George Lamming, Samuel Selvon, and V.S. Naipaul.

Our first face-to-face encounter was at the now famous 1962 Makerere Conference of Writers of English Expression. By then she worked in Uganda, where she lived with her husband, Professor Ogot, who was among the first African professors in Makerere. My maths teacher at Alliance had become my history professor at Makerere. Meanwhile, Grace Ogot had carved a place for herself in the literary sphere.

It was at the Makerere conference that I learned that Grace Ogot and I had another thing in common, apart from our debate at Maseno. At the end of 1961, independently of each other, she and I had submitted novels for the first East African novel writing competition. Mine would later be published as *The River Between* in 1965; hers, as *The Promised Land* in 1966. Our paths would later cross in Kenya, where we launched the Kenya Writers Association, which never got off the ground, caught up as it was by the invisible and unpredictable hand of history.

I was imprisoned by the Kenyatta regime from 1977 to 1978 at Kamĩtĩ Maximum Security Prison, where I wrote my first novel in Gĩkũyũ, *Caitaani Mũtharabainĩ*, later translated into English as *Devil on the Cross*. The novel was published in 1981, along with my play *Ngaahika Ndeenda*, which had put me in prison. That was the same year that Grace Ogot published her first works in Dholuo, *Aloo Kod Apul-Apul* (*Aloo and the Ogre*) and *Ber Wat* (*The Goodness of a Relative*). So, although I was in prison and she outside, we seem to have turned to African languages at about the same time.

A year later, in 1982, I was forced into exile by Daniel Arap Moi. I opposed the dictatorship, working night and day with the London-based Committee for the Release of Political Prisoners in Kenya. Grace worked with the regime, even earning a ministerial position. During the more than twenty years of Moi's reign of terror, she and I never communicated, directly or indirectly. I could understand. Many people were put in prison, a few even tortured after being accused of having met me in London or of having read my books. A few Kenyan intellectuals denounced me, but not Grace Ogot. Still, it was a great divide between us.

When I returned to Kenya in 2003 for the launch of the my Gĩkũyũ-language novel *Mũrogi wa Kagogo* (*Wizard of the Crow*), Grace Ogot was there. She made a big impression on two of my children, Mũmbi wa Ngũgĩ and Thiong'o Kĩmathi. She was still the Grace-ful presence I had met years ago. Naturally, we never talked about the politics of the past, only the politics of writing in African languages. *Miaha*, her third book in Dholuo, was later translated into English as *The Strange Woman* by Duncan Okoth-Okombo, published in 1983, three years before my third novel in Gĩkũyũ, *Matigari ma Njirũngi*, which came out in 1986 only for it to be promptly banned. (The book appeared in English as *Matigari* in 1998, translated by Wangũi wa Goro and published by Africa World Press of Trenton, New Jersey.)

All in all, the parallels between our literary careers were uncanny. Grace Ogot's birth surname, now her middle name, is Akinyi, which means "dawn." It is a name that I gave to a character in my novel *Petals of Blood*, to signify the possibility of the dawn of a new world. But Akinyi also speaks to Grace Ogot's contribution to Kenyan literary culture. She was present at the dawn of Anglophone Kenyan literature, and she established herself as one of the major founders of the modern Kenyan literary tradition.

14
Nadine Gordimer: A Tribute from a Kindred Spirit

"Nadine and Ngugi Arrested in Amherst." No, this was not the case, but that is how my wife, Njeeri, imagined the headlines would be in Kenya and South Africa accompanying the photograph of Gordimer and me entering a police car in the shadow of a heavily armed officer. It was 1991. Both of us were visiting Amherst in Massachusetts at the same time. Although our visits had been scheduled long in advance, Gordimer's presence coincided with the news of her winning the Nobel Prize in Literature. She was not just another visiting writer, but a Nobel laureate. The crowds were curious. Amherst College arranged a police escort, more for her than me, but for joint events we traveled together. Nadine was struck by the irony of the situation and remarked, with a wry smile, that she and I had entered a police car voluntarily. I basked in the reflected glory of her Nobel, I told her, and she deftly deflected by saying it was not yet in her hands.

It was our first one-on-one encounter, but it was as if we had known each other all our lives. It was through books, of course, and some of our books had shared a similar fate in being banned at various times in apartheid South Africa. There was a difference in our literary ages. By the time I wrote my first two, *The River Between* and *Weep Not, Child*, she had already published at least two major novels, *The Lying Days* in 1953 and *A World of Strangers* in 1958, in addition to a significant body of short fiction. She was not at the now famous Conference of African Writers of English Expression at Makerere in 1962, but her name was always in the air. In discussions, Es'kia Mphahlele, Lewis Nkosi, and Arthur Mamaine—writers most closely associated with the Sophiatown Renaissance—always invoked her name in sessions on South African writing. Even at the high noon of apartheid, these writers and their opponents saw her as one of "us."

Sophiatown was a Black suburb of Johannesburg. In the 1950s, it became a vibrant cultural center for writing, music, dancing, and other arts. The period became known as the Sophiatown Renaissance, akin to the Harlem Renaissance in the United States. Blacks were forcibly removed in the 1960s, and the town was rebuilt for whites only under the name Triomf (Triumph). In 2006, its original name was restored, and since then it has become a mixed-race community.

Gordimer was, of course, on the other side of the color line. She could still live in South Africa, her country of birth and upbringing. Many writers were then in exile, and others, such as Alex La Guma and Dennis Brutus, were in prison or under house arrest. While aware that Gordimer did not personally suffer any of these punishments, Black authors acknowledged their kinship with her, which is obvious in their many references. It was during the Conference of African Writers of English Expression that her name became indelibly etched in my mind.

That was in 1962, and in 1991 we met for the first time, not in Africa but America, in sharply contrasting circumstances. The reversal of fortunes was contained in that Amherst ride in a police car in 1991. I was in exile from Moi's dictatorship in postcolonial Kenya, and she was at home in a postapartheid South Africa, symbolized by the recent release of her friend Nelson Mandela after twenty-seven years in prison. Though some of the Sophiatown writers and *Drum* magazine writers like Can Themba and Bloke Modisane had passed on, a good number of the others were now back in South Africa. It was reminiscent of the title of the great documentary *Come Back, Africa,* which captured the spirit of optimism in the resistance culture of the blues and jazz of Sophiatown. In Gordimer's work, including *The Late Bourgeois World* and *Burger's Daughter*, and in her under- and overground support of the liberation movement, she had contributed to that historic "come back," which saw once banned movements now unbanned, and the formerly criminalized principle of one person, one vote now enshrined in the new constitution.

Two years after that first meeting, I visited South Africa to witness the unfolding drama. It was at the courtesy of the newly founded Congress of South African Writers, with Gordimer as its first patron and also its main financial backer. Keorapetse Kgositsile, a recently returned exile, was among my guides in my tour of the different parts of the country meeting with activists of all ages, including with

Nelson Mandela at the African National Congress offices in Johannesburg. Gordimer was away at the time, but through Kgositsile she sent her apologies and message of welcome. In my talks with Kgositsile, Gordimer emerged a major literary character in the drama of the unfolding cultural landscape of the new South Africa at birth. She was one of us.

She wrote a sterling reference for me when, in 2002, the University of California–Irvine, was considering me for the position of Distinguished Professor of English and Comparative Literature and the founding directorship of its International Center for Writing and Translation. When in 2013 the same institution elected to award me the UCI Medal, it again turned to her. She recorded a video tribute that was so touching, it made me teary. It was not just her words, but also her finding the time and the space in her busy life to do this.

Whenever I rewatch it, the video takes me back to our last face-to-face meeting. It was at the 2010 Gothenburg Book Fair, with its jostling but friendly madding crowds. We ran into each other there. She was with her friend Per Wästberg—they were both former presidents of International PEN, an organization that had been instrumental in my release from Kamĩtĩ Maximum Security Prison in Kenya in 1978. We talked briefly, and we both recalled our encounter in Amherst when we rode in a police car together, glorying in the crowning achievement of her long literary life, which began with her first book of short stories, *Face to Face*, released in 1949, when I was two years into elementary school.

She remained true to her art, but she also knew that the

politics of struggle gave energy to her art. She was born on the other side of the color line, but she built bridges across that line. Speaking truth to power was the real power of her art.

She may have passed on, but her ninety years among us are a blessing. For me, her presence and energy are forever alive in my memory. She remains a kindred spirit for, beyond her writing and her activism, she was an unwavering supporter of writing in African languages.

The quantity and quality of her literary output—her short stories, her novels, and her essays—earned her many awards, but in the end, the greatest award was the affection and respect she received from people of all races in South Africa and the world over. Her written words are forever an integral part of the collective memory of the world.

Nadine Rĩtwa Rĩaku Nĩ Mwĩhoko
by Ngũgĩ wa Thiong'o

Nadine witũ rĩtwa rĩaku nĩ mwĩhoko

Waciarĩirwo mũrĩmo wa ũtonga wa gĩkonde
Ũkĩambĩrĩria gwaka ndaraca kũringa mũkuru
O na Abatheindi ya citharia kana gũcicina na rũmena
Wacokaga o ho na karamu na ũmĩrĩru na mwĩhoko

Nadine witũ rĩtwa rĩaku nĩ mwĩhoko

Wakorire mararĩra ũkamagiria maithori
Mahũtie ũkĩmenyũrĩra iria weigĩire

Manyotie ũkĩmakundia marĩa wekuĩire
Maranyarirwo ũkamomĩrĩria na ciugo cia mwĩhoko

Nadine witũ rĩtwa rĩaku nĩ mwĩhoko

Wakorire moyanĩire mabanga
Wee no karamu woiyire na igũrũ
Kĩama gĩkĩringĩka
Karamu hakĩgĩa hinya ũkĩrĩte wa rũhiũ

Nadine witũ rĩtwa rĩaku nĩ mwĩhoko

Ngũkiuga atĩa mũnene gũkĩra ũũ:
Wakorire magĩkua ngoro
Ũkĩmekĩra ngoro na ciugo
Cia Karamu karaita rangi handũ ha thakame.

Nadine witũ rĩtwa rĩaku nĩ mwĩhoko

O na wathiĩ kũrĩa aaMandela marĩ
O na twaga gũkuona na maitho gũkũ thĩ
Nĩ twakũgaya Mwĩhoko wĩ ciugoinĩ ciaku
Iria Watũũra uugaga Mĩaka mĩrongo kenda

Nadine, Your Name Is Hope
Translated from the Gĩkũyũ by Ngũgĩ wa Thiong'o

Dear Nadine, Your Name Is Hope.

You were born on the wealthy side of the color divide.
You built bridges across the divide.
Even when Apartheid destroyed or burnt them down
with hatred,
You went back at it with pen, courage, and hope.

Dear Nadine, Your Name Is Hope.

You found the crying; you wiped their tears.
Those without food, you shared what you had kept
aside.
Those who were thirsty, you shared the water you
carried.
The tortured, you uplifted them with words
of hope.

Dear Nadine, Your Name Is Hope.

You found swords raised;
You just raised your pen.
A miracle came to be.
The pen had power greater than the sword.

Dear Nadine, Your Name Is Hope.

What then remains to say?
You found broken hearts.
You put them back together with words
From a pen that flowed ink instead of blood.

Dear Nadine, Your Name Is Hope.

Even though you're now with Mandela and others,
Even though we don't see you with our earthbound eyes,
We have inherited hope from your words
That you have spun these ninety years.

15

The Three Js: Jomo, Jaramogi, and "James"

I was the reporter on duty one Sunday in the old offices of the *Nation* newspapers in Nairobi way back in 1964 when a call came from Gatundu, the home of Jomo Kenyatta, the first president of Kenya, asking for coverage of a very important event. The news editor assigned me the task. "What is the event?" I asked.

"A ceremony," he said. "Some people have brought donations for the victims of the floods in Kano Plains in Nyanza." The floods that year had indeed been devastating; the wreckage had been prominent in the news. The cameraman on duty and I drove to Gatundu. I had expected to find big donors dishing out tons of money and checks. I was in for a surprise.

Jomo Kenyatta and his vice president, Jaramogi Oginga Odinga, were standing in the compound surrounded not by the donors of my imagination but a crowd of ordinary men and women who had come all the way from Murang'a to contribute whatever they had to ameliorate the suffering of their fellow Kenyans in Nyanza. I had never met either of these two legendary leaders of Kenya's anticolonial politics face to face, let alone the two together. My cameraman managed to capture the only picture in which you'll ever find Jomo Kenyatta, Jaramogi Oginga Odinga, and Ngũgĩ wa Thiong'o together. I then wrote under James Ngugi, a name I would abandon.

Years later, the two would touch my life in different ways. In December 1977, Jomo Kenyatta and Daniel arap Moi imprisoned me for a year at Kamĩtĩ Maximum Security Prison for the work I did with workers and farmers at Kamĩrĩthũ. Jaramogi Oginga Odinga and Achieng Oneko, on the other hand, came to my place in Gitogothi, Limuru, on different days soon after my release in December 1978 to welcome me home from prison. The grassroots education and cultural program at Kamĩrĩthũ spoke to Kenya, Oginga said.

There was more to Jaramogi and me. We were both graduates of Alliance High School, though at different years. We had a common publisher, Heinemann. My book *Weep Not, Child* was one of the African Writers Series, as was his autobiography, *Not Yet Uhuru*. I first read his book as a manuscript in London at the request of Heinemann, who wanted my comments. It was as though I had met him in book form long before I met him in person. In 1968, I resigned from the University of Nairobi in protest at what I saw as government infringement on academic freedom. The state would not allow Jaramogi, as the leader of Kenya People's Union, to speak to the faculty and students. Later he was arrested and imprisoned without charges at Kamĩtĩ Maximum Security Prison. Ten years later, I would be in the same lockup, so there was an element of solidarity in his visit to me.

However, that is not the reason I have kept that picture with me through my years of study abroad in Leeds and teaching in Nairobi, my years of imprisonment, and my twenty-two years of exile in Europe and America—forty-six years altogether. I did not even mention the photograph when, during my years of exile in London, Jaramogi met with Abdilatif Abdalla and me, and briefed him about the work of the Committee for the Release of Political Prisoners in Kenya. Why have I kept it close to me all these years?

It is an image of ordinary men and women from one part of our country extending a helping hand to ordinary men and women from another part of our country. It was a people-to-people declaration of shared pain and hope. This was the picture of the Kenya I had hoped we would build, the Kenya I hope we can still build, a union of Kenyans rooted in the empowerment of the ordinary working men and women of our land. It is a guiding vision in my books.

Unfortunately, we seem to have lost that sense of common hope and deliverance. Nothing exemplifies this today more than the continued existence of internally displaced persons (IDPs). I don't really want to revisit the issue, but among Kenyans abroad it crops up in discussions fairly frequently. IDPs are a continuing reminder of the wound we have inflicted on ourselves. The death of innocents is horrible, no matter the cause, but surely no Kenyan should ever die at the hands of another Kenyan on the basis of their ethnicity. Nobody chooses the biological community into which one is born. Being Luo, Gĩkũyũ, Kamba, or Kalenjin is not a policy or an ideology; it's just a fact of birth. Nobody should ever apologize or feel guilty for being born of a particular biology and culture. Any genuine leadership must take responsibility for each and every Kenyan no matter their regional and biological origins. Political differences will never end, nor should they ever end, for without a clash of ideas and visions, we would always be circling around the same idea, and this would lead to political inbreeding. Let there be a thousand competing visions, but they should be visions of how to effect the empowerment of the poor, the landless, the jobless, the working people, the small-time farmers, the fisher people, and the herders of Kenya. *Ethnicity is not a vision.* In all the years that I and the people I worked with opposed the Moi dictatorship, and in all the hundreds of leaflets we produced and distributed in Kenya and abroad, we never—and I repeat, *never*—blamed it on the Kalenjin people. We always talked about the Moi dictatorship. We knew that the problem was not Moi as a Kalenjin but Moi as a dictator.

At all levels of our society, every effort must be made to heal the wound by ensuring the full restoration of property rights to the victims of our postelection violence. To heal this wound, we don't need permission from the world. It is a Kenyan responsibility as the very first and necessary step in healing. Unfortunately, we in Kenya have a history of amnesia. Mau Mau guerrillas fought for our independence; many died in detention camps. Come independence, we forgot about them. The same for the postindependence deaths of Tom Mboya, J.M. Kariuki, and Robert Ouko. In 1992, people were killed with arrows, and others were driven out of their properties. I remember a grisly photograph of a corpse on the front page of the *Daily* or *Sunday Nation*: the dead person, with several arrows planted in his body, looked like a porcupine. Again, we forgot, only to reenact the carnage that resulted in the current IDPs. If we do not deal with our national wounds, then the wounds will fester inside the soul of the body politic with terrible consequences for the future. Kenyan leaders must use the tragedy as a teaching moment for all Kenyans—teaching by what they do and say.

That's why many Kenyans abroad were excited by the new constitution; they saw it as offering hope for a new Kenya. We still believe that it offers the basis of building internal institutions that can stand the test of political winds and serve as credible arbitrating mechanisms in the event of any crisis. Institutions are the building blocks of a nation, any nation. By building good ones, we Kenyans need never look for justice and restitution from outside our borders.

However, a constitution, though basic and important, is just that: a document to be used to *constitute* a political culture of democracy and human rights. A Kenyan life must be held sacred. Governments and leaders of political parties must be held accountable when they violate the right to life. We should build a political culture wherein such violations are a thing of our colonial past. Leaders must lead, and no leader should talk or behave as if he is at war with another community, or use the word *enemy* to refer to another community. One cannot be a leader and target a community as an enemy. That's like a father who loves some of his children but declares war on the others. No leader should target any community's nonexploitive customs as some kind of political crime.

So far, I have not used the colonial word *tribe*. We should call and refer to communities by the names they call themselves. In every African country, there are only two tribes: the haves and the have-nots. The haves are a very tiny tribe. The have-nots are the vast majority. But haves use the oldest trick in the book of dictatorships: divide and conquer. When it comes to a civil war among the haves over their share of the loot of the nation, they always try to get some of the have-nots to fight a proxy war on their behalf, arming them with machetes, bows and arrows, or guns. They watch the progress of the proxy war from their palaces and hotel suites, sometimes even sharing cocktails as they watch Rome burn.

The gap between the rich and the poor is widening and deepening everywhere. It's the same in Egypt, Libya, and the Ivory Coast, and this gap is the root of all instabilities in Africa. As J.M. Kariuki once warned, you cannot build a successful society of ten millionaires on the shoulders of ten million beggars. Nevertheless, in all our cities, a single skyscraper is surrounded by a sea of shacks. I don't think it is a matter of national pride when Nairobi's Kibera and Mathare are described as the biggest slums in Africa, the haunting grounds of filmmakers in search of shocking scenes. Let all leaders, whatever their party, come up with policies for the have-nots, and they will find that tribe everywhere.

Genuine poverty eradication policies would benefit the poor everywhere. To unite these people, to harness their energies for the common good is the most urgent task of our leadership in Kenya and Africa today. We must make all Kenyans feel that, whenever any child in any part of Kenya goes without food, without school, and without hope, they too are without food, school, and hope. This Kenya of shared hope and common deliverance is what I saw in that photograph of the Murang'a people heeding the cries of the victims of the Kano floods back in 1964, looking up at me, asking me to tell their story of solidarity to the nation and the world.

16

Mandela Memories: An African Prometheus

I first met Nelson Mandela in 1991 in Johannesburg at the offices of the African National Congress during my visit to South Africa as the guest of the Congress of South African Writers to talk at various community centers and share ideas and experiences in the unfolding postapartheid democratic process. Mandela had just resumed the presidency of the ANC after twenty-seven years in prison. I could never have imagined that my very first engagement in the country would be with the legend of the struggle.

Mandela had been part of my literary and political imagination since his days as the Black Pimpernel, who time and again made fools of the pursuing apartheid police. A Makerere student at the time, I had just read Baroness Emma Orczy's novel *The Scarlet Pimpernel*, set during the French Revolution, and it was easy to equate the French Reign of Terror with apartheid and Mandela with Percy, the master of disguises and elusive moves. The real Mandela of the Rivonia Trial, the Robben Island prison, and worldwide celebrity added to the legend. He had been the subject of poetry, politics, and popular performance. In London, I had worked with the ANC in exile. I had even met with the hardworking Oliver Tambo, his legal partner, the one who held together a party that was then dubbed a terrorist organization in the West. Mandela's name was always on the horizon of my being. Now, at last, I was going to meet the man.

I did not know what to expect. For some reason, despite the pictures of him emerging from twenty-seven years in prison, despite indeed the pictures of the man in the world press, I still thought I would see Mandela, the young lawyer, his hair parted in the middle, his cheeks slightly puffed—the Mandela of long ago, the pre-Pimpernel days.

In reality, I met a lean, dark-suited gentleman, whose height dwarfed mine. Was he going to talk about his prison days? Ask me about Kenyan politics? Or simply voice his dreams for a South Africa whose leadership he would soon assume? He didn't ask about any of these things. He talked mostly about books: what African writers had meant to him and his fellow political prisoners, and how books had played a role in buoying their spirits. Books, books, and more books. I felt as if through me he was talking to all writers of the world.

We sat at eye level, one on one, but I didn't realize that he grew on me by the second, a towering presence because he did not try to tower over me. Before I knew it, an hour and half had passed, and he was ready to receive the next visitor.

What stayed with me, as I left for KwaZulu land, was his soft, introspective tone. An incident in my first workshop at a library would make me revisit it. The program was clear: after the library event a few miles from Durban, we were to drive to the graveyard of Albert Luthuli, the former president of the ANC, to pay our respects to his memory. I was in midst of telling a story about Kamĩrĩthũ,[1] the open-air community theater that I had been part of and that had involved workers, small-time farmers, the landless, the jobless, and the power of an awakened consciousness. I saw commotion in the audience. The ANC chief of security who had accompanied us hurried out of the room, unbuttoning his jacket. A gunman from the right-wing Inkatha Freedom Party had been about to enter the hall. They disarmed and arrested him in the nick of time.

My workshop ended abruptly. Our visit to Luthuli's grave was canceled. All those present, including an American envoy, drove in a convoy back to Durban. It was then that I realized that my driver was ANC security, and he told me that his own brother had been murdered by thugs—allegedly some of authoritarian politician Mangosuthu Buthelezi's men—the week before.

After Durban, we went to Port Elizabeth in Eastern Cape. I visited the humble home of one of the ANC cadres. He was a father who seemed to embrace the warmth of his family with gratitude, as if they had been a gift he had not expected. Later, he took me to the back of the house. He did not show it to me, but he pointed to where his AK-47 was hidden. I think he saw himself as a soldier on leave, enjoying a temporary cease-fire with the enemy. He could be called to arms at any time, and he could never be sure of a safe return to his family.

The two incidents brought home to me the meaning of Mandela's introspective tone. The country was literally on the verge of a bloodbath, and he knew it. He held the key to its stability. Despite his calm demeanor, this must have weighed on him.

He held the nation together for the five years that he was president, guided by the realization that there is no room for vengeance in good politics. It is easier to tear down than to build up. In his one term, he showed his faith in the ANC and the people.

I would meet him again after my 2003 Steve Biko Memorial Lecture. The meeting was in Johannesburg again, this time in the offices of Mandela's foundation. By then he had left office, the first Black president of a free South Africa, and Thabo Mbeki had taken over as the second. Mandela was different than in our first meeting, a little bit more effusive. He talked about the contribution of other African countries and Cuba to the struggle. He talked a little bit about his continuing contact with leaders of the world, George W. Bush and Tony Blair in particular. He reminisced about Biko, paying tribute to the role of the Black Consciousness Movement and indeed the role of other political parties in the liberation, mentioning Robert Sobukwe by name. Again, he was so generous in his inclusiveness. The question of his giving the Steve Biko Memorial Lecture came up, and indeed he gave the lecture the following year.

As we were leaving, he stood up and placed his hand on my shoulder. Thus we walked to the door, he leaning on my shoulder. Afterward, I told Xolela Mangcu, my host, how touching that was—walking us to the door with his hand on my shoulder, a gesture almost reminiscent of the image of his long walk to freedom. Xolela laughed, then said, "Sorry. Nothing personal. He does that with people. For support." Yes, he was clearly more frail than the first time we met, but his spirits were still high, and once again his charisma and his towering presence commanded awe and respect rather than demanding it.

The third time would have been in 2004 when he, Ali Mazrui, and I were to be awarded honorary doctorates to mark the renaming and relaunching of the former University of Transkei as Walter Sisulu University. Walter Sisulu, an ANC stalwart, was also Mandela's political and spiritual mentor. My wife, Njeeri, and our two children Mũmbi and Thiong'o were less excited about my doctorate than the fact that they were going to meet Mandela. It was an emotional moment for me because I was returning to Kenya for the first time after twenty-two years of forced exile.

Alas, we never met him. He had come down with something, and he could not make it to the ceremony. He would be given his robes at his home. But a few days later, we had the pleasure of visiting his birthplace, Qunu, where now he rests forever.

His passing, though expected, shocked me. At the back of my mind was always a hope that the man who had cheated death so many times would once more rebound. He remains a towering figure in African and world politics.

Blessed Peace, Mandela

Translated from the Gĩkũyũ by Ngũgĩ wa Thiong'o

Even those who then called him a terrorist
Now acclaim him a freedom fighter.

Those who once wanted him gone
Are now shedding tears that he's gone.

It is said that truth never dies.
It cannot be buried in a hole.

They tried to kill it with bullets.
They wondered, how did it escape?

They put it in chains.
They sent it to Rob'em Island.
They made it break stones twenty seven years.
They tortured it to make truth give up hope.
They tried all to make truth surrender to lies.
They did not realize it was the body breaking stones,
That truth cut through the handcuffs and barbed wire long ago,
That it was truth that guided the armed struggle,
Singing that which had been sung by other seekers of freedom.

You can send us to exile and prisons
Or confine us to islands,
But we shall never stop struggling for freedom. . . .

Mandela Madiba Rolihlahla of Thembu and African clan,
Your body that has gone to rest under the shades of holy peace.

The truth they tried to shoot down with bullets,
The truth they put in hand and leg chains,
The truth for which they put you in jail and detention—
That truth lives on among the people for ever
In the hearts of all fighters for truth and justice the world over.

17
Mandela Comes Home

When Mandela was released from prison, a milestone captured in the iconic picture of his walking hand in hand with Winnie Mandela, I wrote an article in Gĩkũyũ, "Kũngũ Baba Mandela" (Welcome Home, Father Mandela), because I could not see myself recording this moment in any but an African language.

On February 11, 1990, watched by thousands gathered in Cape Town and by millions on their television screens around the world, Nelson Mandela walked hand in hand with his wife, Winnie, to freedom and triumph, writing the date into world history. When he spoke, he brought joy to those who listened as he reaffirmed his belief in the people of South Africa and in the principles for which he had been prepared to die—his belief in a democratic, nonracial, and unified South Africa.

Nine days earlier, when F.W. de Klerk announced that Mandela would be free, a nine-year-old girl I know greeted the news by jumping up and down and urging her mother, "Please, let's make a big card and send it to Mandela. It's say,

'Welcome home, Baba Mandela!' " The girl and her mother lived in Newark, and in 1963, when Mandela was jailed for life, the mother Kenyan had been only a baby. Quite clearly, Mandela is in the minds and hearts of several generations—all of whom value human freedom—in Africa and the world.

Why have Mandela's name and personality captivated so many people? He was not the only prisoner. Indeed, many political detainees died in the prisons of South Africa. Others were massacred before the eyes of the world: in Sharpeville in 1960 and in Soweto in 1976. In fact, for the Black people of South Africa, the whole country was one vast prison, particularly in the years of pass laws and passbooks.

The most compelling thing about Mandela is how he endured those years of solitary confinement and other torture without ever surrendering to the racist vampires. In him people see the infinite capacity of the human spirit to resist and to conquer. Do we not for the same reason identify in literature with characters like Prometheus? And in history with people like Paul Robeson, Kwame Nkrumah, Ho Chi Minh, Nat Turner, Toussaint Louverture, Kenyan freedom fighter Dedan Kĩmathi, Zimbabwean resistance leader Mbuya Nehanda, and martyred Chilean poet and singer Víctor Jara?

All these figures are heroic because they reflect more intensely in their individual souls the souls of their community. Their uniqueness is the uniqueness of the historical moment. They make history even as history makes them. They are torches that blaze new paths. Each torch has been lit by the fire of the masses, and every time the flame seems to fade, the great ones turn to their people for more energy.

Mandela has been such a torch for the South African people. The people of South Africa are reflected in Mandela.

In Mandela, people around the world have been applauding the courage, the endurance, the resistance, and the spirit of the South African masses. People around the world, particularly Africans and those of African descent outside Africa, have seen themselves reflected in the struggling South African masses. Or put another way, Mandela is to Black South Africa's struggles what Black South Africa's struggles are to the democratic forces of the world in the twentieth century. Indeed, South Africa is a mirror of the modern world in its emergence over the last four hundred years.

A bold claim? Not really. When Vasco da Gama landed at the Cape of Good Hope in 1498, he not only found for Western Europe an easier route to India's riches, but he also started the long era of Africa's unequal and unwilling partnership in the development of Europe and the newly discovered Americas. Europe's two greatest political economists and philosophers, Adam Smith and Karl Marx, agree in their writings that the "discovery" of the sea route to India via South Africa and of the continent of America were the two most important events in the emergence, growth, and development of post-Renaissance Europe. Smith called them "the two greatest and most important events in the history of mankind." Marx described them as opening up "fresh ground for the rising bourgeoisie" and as giving to trade, commerce, and industry "an impulse never before known."

South Africa, though farthest removed from Europe, became Europe's gateway to the heart of the African continent.

South Africa also became the knot that tied together the diverse histories and fortunes of Asia, Europe, and the United States. Like the rest of the continent, South Africa saw her people hunted down and carried away as slaves. Their labor was used to develop what later became the United States, and profits from the sale of their bodies as commodities became part of the capital that figures such as W.E.B. Du Bois, C.L.R. James, and Eric Williams have proved was the basis of Western Europe's nineteenth-century industrial revolution.

From 1652, when first Dutch and French settlers, then British settlers streamed into South Africa and began forcibly taking land from the Africans, to the nineteenth century, when the whole country became first a British colony and then a neocolony supervised by a white minority, the gold, diamonds, and mineral resources of South Africa were used to develop Western European industries—and later U.S. industry, too—and to build enormous gold reserves. Is there any bank, financial institution, or industry of any significant size in Western Europe, the United States, and Japan that is not indebted to the gold and diamonds of South Africa?

The majority of the industries inside South Africa are branches, subsidiaries, or partners of those in the West, and their enormous profits are clearly rooted in the slave wages of Black workers and in the poverty of the majority guaranteed by the cruel system of apartheid. The South African economy is still inextricably tied to that of the West, so it is unsurprising that even now Britain and the United States are hostile to calls for economic boycotts to motivate the South African government and institutions to undo the legacy of apartheid in the country's continued social inequality and Black poverty. To respond to such calls would be to institute boycotts against themselves. In fact, calls for a boycott only began to have some kind of effect when many people in the United States realized that the pillars of apartheid were right at their door—in their financial institutions, in their universities, and in their industries—and they started calling for disinvestment. Collectively, they brought pressure on their government and their business communities.

In the South African system, people see the bitter fruition of at least five forces that have bedeviled the development of human beings: classical colonialism, neocolonialism, slave wages, racism, and the usurpation of the people's sovereignty through the denial of democracy.

But Black South Africans are not endlessly helpless victims of superior forces. Their history presents a people who have been pioneers in the struggle for communal survival, national liberation, and social emancipation. The ferocity of Black South African resistance blunted the determined efforts of European settlers to annihilate them. Shaka, the great king of the Zulu, is possibly the best known of all the leaders of pre-twentieth-century resistance in Africa, and his name continues to inspire liberation efforts.

Black South Africa has had to pay a high price for its resistance. From Shaka to Mandela, its people experienced one massacre after another at the hands of Europeans. The Sharpeville and Soweto massacres remind African people of other massacres in colonial African history: at the Hola Camp in Kenya, in Wiriyamu in Mozambique, in Algiers in Algeria, and the massacres of the Herero people in Namibia. But the Black people of South Africa have never given up hope.

There have been other pioneering successes in Black South Africa. The African National Congress, formed in 1912, is one of the oldest modern political parties in Africa. The ANC can be described as the father and mother of all other African liberation movements. Its anthem, "Nkosi Sikelel' iAfrika" (God Bless Africa), is the nearest thing to a Pan-African internationale, and its melody is now the national anthem of Tanzania and Zimbabwe. Furthermore, Africa is not the only beneficiary of the pioneering liberation struggles of the Black South African people. Mahatma Gandhi of India started his political activism in South Africa, and the independence of India in 1948 inspired independence movements throughout the rest of Asia and Africa.

The one thing that makes all Africans and all Black people around the world see themselves reflected in the history of the Black South African people, and therefore of Mandela, is the global fight against racism and the color line, once described by W.E.B. Du Bois as the problem of the twentieth century. Racial oppression carries within it many forms of denial—economic, political, cultural, and psychological. Who does not see themselves reflected in that mirror?

South Africa is me. South Africa is you. South Africa is all the Black people of the Earth. South Africa is all the workers of the world. South Africa is all of humanity in its struggle to save itself. If that struggle for the recovery of a sense of human community is led by South Africa's masses through their political organizations, like the South African Communist

Party, the ANC, and the Pan-African Congress, it is equally true that Nelson Mandela has been its leading symbol. He has firmly held aloft the mirror in which the twentieth century has been looking at itself.

I hope that his release, coming as it did in the closing decade of the twentieth century, amid so many changes in the power map of the world and amid the calls to give power to the people, will come to be seen as only one step to the liberation of the Black South African people, so that they can control their economy, their politics, and their culture. Whether they achieve that kind of empowerment or not will depend on the extent to which they can resist being pressured by the West to accept the Kenya solution. In 1962, Jomo Kenyatta was released from eight years in prison, and he proceeded to negotiate away everything that the Kenya Land and Freedom Army (the Mau Mau) had fought for. Colonial structures were left intact, and Kenya under Daniel arap Moi became one of the most repressive states in the world, a neocolony completely and pathetically dependent on the West. Kenyatta lost on the negotiating table what had already been won on the battlefield by the Kenyan people.

Black South Africa cannot accept, or indeed afford, to replace the 1910 neocolonial arrangement run by a white minority with a perpetual neocolonial arrangement run by a Black minority. The history of the last four hundred years calls upon them to overthrow the triple burdens of colonialism, neocolonialism, and racial oppression and to start on a genuine march toward justice for all.

Mandela's release is his own victory and the victory of the

ANC and the other liberation movements. It is also the victory of the Black South African people and of all Black and African peoples, and the victory of all lovers of human freedom. Mandela's example teaches us that people around the world must redouble their support for liberation movements in their quest for independence and freedom. Perhaps the nine-year-old girl was so excited about Mandela's release because in it she caught a glimpse of the future, as it will be created by generations determined to ensure that the twenty-first century will be the century of Africa and of all exploited and oppressed people of the Earth.

18
Henry Chakava: A Model of Development in Africa

I

I graduated from Kamĩtĩ Maximum Security Prison on December 12, 1978, with the manuscript of a novel, written on toilet paper in Gĩkũyũ, under the title: *Caitaani Mũtharabainĩ*. In the novel, I had played with the idea that it was not Christ who should have been executed on the cross but the Devil himself. Jesus was an opponent of Roman imperialism, a proponent of the least among us, a visionary who saw the poor, among whom he walked, as inheriting the earth. The Devil was an ally of Roman imperialism and its oppressive practices, a self-serving criminal whose followers, exploiters of the poor, have as much chance of entering heaven as a camel through the eye of a needle.

Writing the novel had made me better able to cope with life in solitary confinement, almost as if, with a stolen pen and stolen toilet paper, I was in daily combat against the forces that had incarcerated me. But a manuscript, no matter the cirumstances in which it comes to be, is just an incomplete project until it reaches the reader through a publisher. The publisher is the most crucial link between the writer and the reader. Would my publisher want to publish a Gĩkũyũ-language novel?

Henry Chakava was then the head of Heinemann Kenya, a branch of the U.K.-based firm of the same name. In 1962, Heinemann had come up with the brilliant idea of an African Writers Series (AWS). Beginning with Chinua Achebe's *Things Fall Apart*, the list had turned African writing in English and European languages into a global phenomenon. But despite the name and the phenomenal growth, the AWS had never published anything in an African language, only Europhone African literature. Their branches, in Nigeria and Kenya, had followed suit. Up until my arrest and imprisonment, I had faithfully followed that model: I was Anglophone. My novels *The River Between*, *Weep Not, Child*, *A Grain of Wheat*, and *Petals of Blood* were in the Europhone tradition.

I was in a dilemma. The Moi regime had taken over the reigns of power from Jomo Kenyatta, who had passed on three months earlier. The new regime had kept us "illegally" in prison for those three months. By their own laws, the new leader was supposed to set us free on the death of the president, under whom I had been imprisoned without trial. He could retain us a day longer only under new detention orders. I was also aware that, although it was Jomo Kenyatta who had imprisoned me, it was Daniel arap Moi, then home minister, who had signed the order for my imprisonment, a punishment for my having co-written the play *Ngaahika Ndeenda* in Gĩkũyũ, and having it performed by Kamĩrĩthũ. I knew that the new Moi regime was no less hostile to my writing in an African language, my own in particular. Now I had come out of prison with yet another major work in Gĩkũyũ and was going to ask Henry Chakava to do something that Heinemann publishers had never done before: bring out a novel in Gĩkũyũ, a language that had never had a novel published in it before. For those reasons, I was hesitant to approach Chakava.

I should not have been. Chakava never even raised any of my concerns as a problem. He was going to publish the novel, and he was going to give it the same kind of editorial resources that he had given my Anglophone works. Indeed, he saw this as the opening chapter of publishing in African languages. He had already shown his commitment in that direction by having all the major African writers at the time translated into Kiswahili, against the grain of the original Europhone African Writers Series. The word went out: he was going to publish a novel that I had written in Kamĩtĩ.

Then came the real test to his commitment: Chakava started getting anonymous telephone threats. They intensified as the publication date approached. Their frequency and intensity did not slow Chakava.

A week before publication, assassins waited for him at the gate of his house in Lavington, a suburb of Nairobi. They tried to force him into the trunk of their car, but an approaching motorist foiled the plot. One of the attackers thought of finishing the job on the spot and swung a machete at Chakava's head. He raised his hand as a shield, and the assassin cut off one of his fingers before the attackers fled the scene. The finger had to be reattached.

Alarmed about his safety, those in the Heinemann London office asked him to abandon the project. Though I was keen that the novel come out, I did not want Chakava to risk his life over a book. I let him know that whatever he decided to do, I would understand. He did not say yes or no. He just pressed ahead with his plans to publish the novel.

The failed abduction and the near loss of his finger did not deter him. *Caitaani Mũtharabainĩ* (later translated into English as *Devil on the Cross*) came out as scheduled, in 1981, alongside the play *Ngaahika Ndeenda*.

It is in keeping with Chakava's character that he hardly ever talks about his defiance and courage. Twenty-four years later, when I invited him to give a lecture at the International Center for Writing and Translation at the University of California–Irvine, on publishing in African languages, I had to coax him to talk about it. His attitude was simply that he was a publisher, he had accepted the novel on its own merit as a literary text and not as a pretext to make an ideological statement or heroic stand. The threats had challenged his integrity as a publisher, and he had stood by that integrity.

That was not the end of the saga of the challenges he faced in publishing my Gĩkũyũ-language works. Following my return home from prison, the Kamĩrĩthũ Community Education and Cultural Center planned to put on a production of *Maitũ Njugĩra*, another of my Gĩkũyũ-language plays, not at Limuru but at the Kenya National Theater. Chakava helped us book the theater by paying in advance for all the days and times of our run. The effort ended with the doors of the national theater locked and armed police patrolling the area, some in full riot gear in formation at the Central Police Station, ready to attack. This time, Chakava received no threats or any attempts on his life, but he never recovered the money he had paid.

To ensure that Kamĩrĩthũ would never again pose any challenges, the regime sent three trucks of armed police to the center and razed the original open-air stage to the ground. Theater in the area was banned. Later, in 1982, in London, for the launch of the *Devil on the Cross*, I learned that, after the attempted coup by members of the Kenya Air Force, a "red" carpet awaited me on my return. I was forced into exile.

The obvious parallel between prison and exile is being forced away from home, and I reacted to both in a similar fashion. In prison I had written a Gĩkũyũ-language novel; in exile, I wrote another novel in Gĩkũyũ in a completely English-language environment. In *Matigari ma Njirũngi*, I further experimented with the narrative structures of oral tales in theme and form. The theme of the quest served me well because I was challenging the culture of silence and fear prevailing in Kenya under the Moi regime. What about a character who breaks that silence by questioning members of different social classes? As for the form, what about the repetition so common in oral tales? *Matigari* was to my exile what *Devil on the Cross* was to my prison. Writing them in trying conditions was my way of fighting back, and frankly bolstering my own spirits.

Once again came the question of publishing the novel. It was obvious that it had to be done in Kenya. No English publisher would undertake to bring out a book in an

African language. Even if there had been such a publisher, he would have had to face the fact there were hardly any Gĩkũyũ-language readers in Europe. He would have to be committed enough to print it in London and then export it to Kenya.

But repression in Kenya had intensified. Effigies of me were being burned in the streets on order of the regime. "Rumor mongering," both in private and in public, had become a crime. Dreaming about the possible death of the president had long been criminalized. Once again, I turned to Henry Chakava.

He brought it out in Kenya in 1986 to an incredible reception by the reading public. In a short time, the fearless, daring character Matigari, who went around the country asking questions about truth and justice, became a legend.

The government's reaction was completely unexpected. Horrified by intelligence reports that there was a man going about the country asking such questions and spreading "rumors" at a time when rumor mongering had been criminalized, the Moi regime set out to arrest Matigari. On realizing that he was a fictional character, they went for the book itself. A police squad raided all the bookshops in the country, as well as the publisher's warehouse, taking all copies of the book. Fortunately, Chakava was not harmed.

The next act in this saga involved *Mũrogi wa Kagogo*, translated into English as *Wizard of the Crow*. It was another novel written in exile. I started it at some point in 1996, almost ten years after *Matigari*. I was then the Erich Maria Remarque Professor of Languages and also Professor of Comparative

Literature and Performance Studies at New York University, although I lived in New Jersey. It was quite a task. The story took control of me, and I followed it as it wandered all over the imaginary territory of Aburiria. But it went beyond Aburiria to Asia and America, and it was a relief when about six years later I had contained it into a book.

I have always joked that *Mũrogi wa Kagogo* has the unique quality of being the only novel in history ever written between two oranges. This is because I began writing it in Orange, New Jersey, and completed it in Orange County, California, where I moved in 2002 as Distinguished Professor of English and Comparative Literature and Director of the International Center for Writing and Translation, at the University of California–Irvine. It was at the ICWT that Henry Chakava gave a seminar on publishing in African languages. By then, the political climate in Kenya had changed dramatically. The Moi dictatorship had been replaced by a kind of multiparty democracy, and this had ushered in a new leader, Mwai Kĩbaki, my former professor of economics from my undergraduate days at Makerere in the colonial 1960s.

It was during his visit to Irvine that Chakava and I started talking about my return to Kenya. I would go back home as the guest of East African Educational Publishers, but we agreed that my return, whenever it happened, should climax with the launching of the new novel, *Mũrogi wa Kagogo.* Such a launch would be a fitting crown for my return home after twenty-three years in forced exile. When the moment came in 2003, Henry Chakava sought to organize the activities around the theme of reviving the spirit. This was meant as a tribute to the renaissance spirit of the 1970s in the University of Nairobi's Department of Literature. It was a period of dynamic public lectures, when artists and writers exiled from Uganda, Malawi, and South Africa congregated in Nairobi. Despite the creeping authoritarianism, it was a decade of optimism before dictatorship and darkness descended on the land and a culture of silence and fear reigned. The renaissance became a distant memory of what we could have become.

On a personal level, I was returning to a Kenya where my mother, Wanjiku, and my first wife, Nyambura, had died without my being able to bury them. My "other mothers" and members of the extended family who had been part of my youth had similarly passed on. "Reviving the spirit" *was* what drove my return home after twenty-three years of exile. Along with me were my wife Njeeri, and my youngest children, Mũmbi and Thiong'o. Like me, Njeeri and the children were all looking forward to the launch of the novel they had seen me struggle with from 1996 to 2003. Mũmbi and Thiong'o went to stay with their aunt in Mang'u, but they would be back in Nairobi on the night of the launch. A week before the launch of *Mũrogi wa Kagogo*, four armed gunmen broke into our hotel room and savagely attacked my wife and me. Like Chakava in 1982, we barely escaped with our lives. Was this the "red" carpet that I had been warned about back in 1982?

We debated whether to flee our country once again and go back to my country of exile. Despite the trauma, Njeeri and I agreed that we would not let them drive us out of Kenya, that we would not give them the satisfaction of flight. The launch of *Mũrogi wa Kagogo* would go on as scheduled.

Chakava would have completely understood had we decided to abandon the launch. Once we agree to continue, he became even more determined to see it through and ensure that terror did not kill our spirit.

On looking back, there seems to have been a pattern, a conscious, dogged attempt to prevent an African-language literary enterprise.

Yet despite that pattern of violence, a pattern in some ways reminiscent of similar violence against producers of African-language newspapers, poems, and songs during the the State of Emergency of the 1950s, the modern Gĩkũyũ-language novel was born. More important, Chakava launched a program of publishing in African languages other than Kiswahili. Chakava was the publishing mind behind the reemergence of the still struggling African-language publishing scene in post-colonial Kenya.

II

I have known Chakava for many years now, and our relationship has gone through many transformations. He was my student before he became my publisher. This was at the University of Nairobi, where I taught from 1968 to 1969 and from 1972 to 1977. In my time, the department changed from being the Department of English, which was centered on English national literature, to the Department of Literature, which was centered on Africa in the context of world literature.

Chakava was one of the many brilliant products of the latter. I remember him as the student who clocked A's in all his papers in all his subjects with all his teachers. His First Class Degree was not a surprise. Chakava could have gone on to become an outstanding academic, writing books for other scholars to read, but he chose the path of a publisher, ensuring that what others wrote reached the reading public. In so doing, he came to shape the production of knowledge in Kenya and East Africa, becoming a pioneer in book production by Africans for Africa. In the process, he nurtured many young talents, including John Kiriamiti, and lured them into the industry.

His role as a pioneer has been recognized with many awards, including an honorary doctorate from Oxford. Henry Chakava became the leading publisher in the continent, a visionary and a model of an Africa-centered publishing enterprise.

The Heinemann Kenya publishing house that Chakava joined soon after college was in every way a branch of the main office in London. The majority of shareholders were based in London. It published texts already approved in London, often a local reprint of what had been published there. Technically Chakava was fulfilling a vision centered on the parent company in London. In a few years, he started initiating Kenya-based publishing ideas. And in the end, the majority of shareholders became Kenyan, eventually buying out the British shareholders and turning the company into a wholly Kenyan enterprise. This was reflected in the change of name: from Heinemann Kenya to East African Educational Publishers. In some ways, this is his legacy for Kenya and Africa. He created a model of how an Africa emerging from years of colonial and imperialist economic domination can develop—a model of national development. To understand the implications of the Chakava model, we have to put what he did in the context of colonial history and the colonial mode of production.

III

The first act and indeed the signal victory of colonial capitalism was the destruction of the African artisan class. These were the workers in iron, copper, and gold. These artisans made things with the raw materials around them. They made jewelry: copper rings to decorate legs, arms, and necks, as well as earrings. They were the minds and hands behind the defense industry, making spears, arrowheads, and swords. They made cooking utensils. Their tools sustained the textile industry, making clothes out of leather and the bark of trees. All industrial growth around the world has been a development of that tradition and that class, which has continuously learned from previous experience or through contact with innovations from other countries, whether friendly or hostile. You build on tradition; you do not destroy it, as did colonial capitalism to African genius and self-belief.

In short, colonialism disabled the class that used to make things for use and exchange from the raw materials around them. Colonial domination killed that tradition of invention and manufacture. The newcomers coerced the export of raw materials to their home countries, where their own artisan class made things out of these same raw materials. They took our gold, copper, and diamonds by force or trickery to fuel their own inventions and manufacturing. The genius of imperialism, aka colonial capitalism, was how it stole our raw materials or got them very cheaply, sometimes for the price of fake beads, and then sold what they had made out of our raw materials back to us at higher price. That was how Africa was turned into an exporter of raw materials and an importer of finished goods. This was basically the system that Africa inherited and even nationalized at independence.

The publishing industry followed the same neocolonial route. Africans wrote, they exported what they wrote to European publishers, who processed the literary raw material and bound it into books, which they then sent back to African schools and colleges. In so doing, they controlled the content that shaped our minds. It was a cultural reflection of what was happening at the economic level. That was the prevailing practice when Chakava took over and changed the foreign-owned Heinemann Kenya into the Kenyan-owned and -run East African Educational Publishers, not by forcible nationalization but by buying out the foreign shareholders.

Today, East African Educational Publishers, fully owned and run by Africans, is one of the largest publishing houses in Africa. The company's pride and self-confidence were on full display during the celebration of the fiftieth anniversary of *Weep Not, Child*'s publication, but it was also celebrating its own fifty years of existence. Although Chakava left the day-to-day work of the company to his managing director and the manager's team, he must have been very pleased to see how the company he had shaped was covered so widely in Kenyan media as a Kenyan institution. It was symbolic that the fiftieth anniversary of *Weep Not Child*, the first novel by a Kenyan African, coincided with the fiftieth anniversary of the company and the fiftieth anniversary of Kenya's independence.

While the original London-based African Writers Series has ended, East African Educational Publishers has been able to keep many of its books alive in English and in translation, while also finding new writers and publishing new titles, as well as mapping new directions in education and publishing. Trusting in Kenya and Africa, Chakava came up with products made in Africa that he could sell in Africa and abroad.

That's why I call Chakava's model an alternative to what has been followed by African governments and policymakers. These policymakers have continued the colonial model, in which Africa rents her resources to the West—raw materials in exchange for finished goods made from them. When they are able to charge a few more dollars for these raw materials, when they invite foreign corporations to manufacture goods in Africa and then sell them there, when they depend on foreign expertise and on foreign NGOs, they call it development. Walter Rodney called it the development of underdevelopment.

The results of such "development," often championed by African governments, are there for all to see. Africa remains the poorest continent. Go to any capital in the Western world and look at any street, and you will not find a single African-owned bank, African-owned trading company, or African-owned industry. You will not find an African-made vehicle.

It is the very opposite in the streets of any African capital. Banks, insurance companies, manufacturing companies, large hotel chains, oil companies, mining companies—these and more are owned by foreign corporations, even when they carry African names and are fronted by African directors. We bend over backward to make local conditions conducive to foreign investors. What about bending over backward to create conditions for local enterprise? Foreign NGOs, funded by foreign governments, run our social services, in the process strengthening dependency instead of independence and self-reliance.

The Chakava model is the only one that can enable Africa to catch up with the West and surpass it. Africa should aim at nothing less than surpassing the exhausted West in everything: manufacture, invention, and good governance in service to humanity's march to a better and more humane future.

IV

He was once my student, whose papers I graded. Then he became my publisher, who graded my manuscripts. Most important, he became a friend, who has stood by me in times of happiness and sorrow, even in those times when being seen with me was dangerous.

Time and again, I have found refuge in Chakava's house. He and his wife and family never seemed to mind that, in giving my family refuge, they were putting themselves in danger.

As my publisher, he has never tried to distance himself from me. Even when my effigies were being burned under the Moi regime, and even some Kenyan academics and former colleagues were denouncing me, or at least distancing themselves from me and my work, Chakava never wavered as my publisher. He was even questioned as to whether my royalties were financing my dissident activities abroad. Dissidence was the state's interpretation of my work with the London-based Committee for the Release of Political Prisoners in Kenya during my exile, when I traveled around the world to expose Moi's reign of terror.

Henry Chakava was never directly or indirectly involved in my political activities, unless it was to ensure that my family got their dues from royalties as per my request, but he never wavered in his professional relationship with me as my publisher. And while he subjected all my manuscripts to the normal procedure, first sending them out for readers' reports and never treating them any differently than other manuscripts.

In a fundamental sense, Chakava has been a great friend to Kenya and Africa. Nothing shows that friendship better than his steering the East African Educational Publishers from an enterprise beholden to foreign interests into one beholden to Kenya and Africa. What heights could Africa not reach, were she to control her own natural resources, manufacture goods with them, and then trade with others accordingly?

This calls for a mental revolution, which starts with a belief in the capacity of the African people to take control of their destiny instead of leaving it to foreign NGOs and corporations. Though still struggling from ferocious competition from better-funded foreign corporations, East African Educational Publishers did it, connecting with the world from a base in Kenya. Others can do it. Hopefully, African states will come up with policies and mind-sets that encourage and support a national innovative entrepreneurship that works from its base in Africa. At seventy, Henry Chakava can proudly say that he has played his part and shown the way.

19

Call Her Molara O: Pioneer in Dialectical African Feminism

Letter writing, personal and public, used to be quite normal. This form is not as dominant today, and there are very few contemporary scholars and writers who can claim that their letters and poetic exchanges have contributed to thought and theory. That's why the friendly poetic exchange between a Nigerian, Molara Ogundipe, and a Malawian, Felix Mnthali, is unique in contemporary Africa. It has added mightily to African literary and feminist thought. I certainly have found it insightful and have cited some of that exchange in my work. The credit goes to Molara O—poet, feminist, critic, and activist—for her uncanny ability to tease out theory from letters between friends. It is a testament to her brilliance.

News of that brilliance reached me long before I met her or read her work. It was through the late Ime Ikiddeh, my fellow postgraduate student at the University of Leeds in the early 1960s. Ikiddeh had graduated from the University of Ghana and I, from Makerere, both affiliates of the University of London. Being products of the English education system, we would know the significance of getting first-class bachelor of arts degrees from London. It was an achievement attainable only to a very few, and Molara O had done it in 1963 at Ibadan, also an affiliate of London. She was the only one in a class of ten. Even before college, she had already signaled her brilliance by graduating from Queen's College, a girls' secondary school, with seven distinctions in her subjects, including science and Latin.

Her performance at Queen's could be seen as a reflection of the cultural broad-mindedness of her mother, Toya Ogundipe. "She read novels, the Bible, foreign and Nigerian magazines, newspapers, and pamphlets," Molara O wrote. "She read Jane Austen and the Brontë sisters with my sister and me. I had read George Eliot, and so many others, before I went to Queen's School. She made sure that she gave all five of us her children a fine education that she believed in strongly and that was cultural for her in a full-bodied way and not simply literacy. Four of us became university professors."[1]

Molara O comes from a remarkable intellectual family, but it was that First Class in English in 1963 that launched her name beyond the borders of her family, her school, her college, and even her country, and into the intellectual firmament of the time. She also became the subject of rumor and hearsay.

Later, over the years, I would meet with her in many places—Nairobi, London, New York, at conferences mostly—where we would always carve out some time to chat. She was among over two hundred scholars from Africa, Asia, Europe,

Canada, and the United States who in April 1994 gathered at the Penn State Berks Campus in Reading, Pennsylvania, to celebrate my work. Even there, we carved out a moment for one or two anecdotes.

We met at conferences, or outside the old Heinemann offices on Bedford Street, or in other London streets, or in the corridors of the University of Nairobi. Our talks would quickly turn to theory and then to anecdotes or stories.

She had a flair for storytelling. Once, at his house near Temple University in Philadelphia, Molefi Asante hosted a group of us, including poet Sonia Sanchez, as well as Njeeri wa Ngũgĩ, my wife, and some of our children. There was plenty of Afrocentricity to go round. In the process, Molara O jolted the gathering into a memorable collective storytelling session. She opened the story with a couple of sentences, to which others would add, beginning with the guest next to her. The story ended up having a fairly coherent trajectory about a character who was born in Africa and moved to Philadelphia. He eventually becomes a soldier and is sent to fight in Vietnam. He survives the fighting and returns to America, where he earns a dishonorable discharge for opposing the war and citing Malcolm X and Muhammad Ali on the commonality of the Vietnamese and the Black community as an oppressed people. It was the art of improvisation at its best, and it illuminated the Afrocentric journey in a lighthearted way at that dinner table.

My most memorable encounter with Molara O, because it was personal and so close to home, was at my house on Berkeley Avenue in Orange, New Jersey, where she engaged with my family nearly all day and night. She was then a visiting distinguished professor in an endowed chair at Rutgers University, one of many campuses in the United States, Europe, and Africa at which she would teach and lecture. That night she did not have to rush to the airport for the next flight, which gave us time for a long, sustained talk, during which we traded memories of common acquaintances and histories. A shared colonial history often gives rise to not-so-unexpected coincidences, like the fact that, at university, Molara O had once played the part of Cordelia in *King Lear*. A production of that play at my school in Kenya remains ingrained in me. The only difference was that with us at Alliance, Cordelia and all her sisters were played by boys. For all practical purposes, schools in Nigeria and Kenya were interchangeable with those in any other parts of the British Empire. Alliance High in Kenya was more or less a version of King's and Queen's colleges, as in Nigeria. So also the universities and colleges from the British West Indies, through Ghana, Nigeria, Uganda, and Kenya, to India, Malaysia, Hong Kong, and Singapore. Our English syllabi in Makerere and Ibadan were modeled on those in London, and that's how Molara and I, from our different countries in Africa, graduated in 1963 with degree certificates from the University of London, or as she put it to me in a recent email, she got her "first class from London because our papers were marked in London and we had external examiners come from London."[2] MADE IN ENGLAND was branded on everything from our clothes and our silverware to our minds.

The English Department of Ibadan was famous, not only

for its academic leadership, including Molly Mahood, Geoffrey Axworthy, Martin Banham, and Ulli Beier, but also for producing a group of writers and intellectuals who would become influential in Africa and around the world. Among these were Chinua Achebe, who five years after his graduation in 1953 published *Things fall Apart*; Wole Soyinka who, years later, would become the first Black African Nobel laureate in literature; Abiola Irele, who would become a leading critical voice in African and Caribbean thought; and J.P. Clark, poet, dramatist, and oraturist, and historically significant as the first editor of *The Horn*.

The Horn, a student-run literary journal, was the brainchild of the young Martin Banham, who, as a graduate student in Leeds from 1952 to 1955, where Wole Soyinka would join him as an undergraduate, was involved in the launch of the Leeds-based cyclostyled poetry magazine *Poetry and Audience*. On joining the faculty at Ibadan in 1956, Banham looked for something similar, and he launched *The Horn* from the English Department in 1957, with the department's cyclostyle machine as the printer, his own £10 as funding, and J.P. Clark as the first editor. It would become a literary horn of plenty.[3] It is interesting that about the same year, at Makerere, *Penpoint*, also cyclostyled, was born. Both *The Horn* and *Penpoint* would spawn many student writers who would go on to become leading literary voices of postcolonial Africa.

Coincidentally, *Black Orpheus*, brainchild of Ulli Beier, was launched the same year. Beier was also among the minds behind the foundation of the Mbari Writers and Artists Club in 1961. *Black Orpheus* was to Nigeria and Africa what

Transition, founded by Rajat Neogy, was to Uganda and Africa. Mphahlele's Chemchemi Cultural Center and Elimo Njau's *Paa ya Paa*, both based in Nairobi, would come later.

Molara O was among those scholars and writers cutting their literary teeth on *The Horn* and probably more significantly on *Black Orpheus* and the Mbari writers clubs. Her relationship with *The Horn* was as a contributor and also one of its editors, which position was passed down yearly among the students of the English Department. She was the editor of *The Horn* in Nigeria the same year that I was editor of *Penpoint* in Uganda. She was also a member of *Black Orpheus* and published in that journal.

"It was easy for me to move around the *Black Orpheus* world," she told me, "not only for my zest and interest then, but also for having met Ulli Beier in Ede, ten miles to Osogbo, where he later established himself with a wide impact. I was a secondary school student then in Ede, at Queen's School, in the late '50s. I used to visit Ulli Beier and Susan Wenger, to whom he was then married. I was fascinated by the respect and love they had for Yoruba culture and knowledge, which attitude found resonance in me from my early education and my missionary parents, whose generation believed in and worked hard to preserve and teach African culture, especially the Yoruba, through school curricula, textbooks, church material."[4]

Molara O attended all the events of the Mbari club and often had lunches there with visiting artists, both national and international, among them African American singers and writers, and Caribbean and Sudanese visual artists. There were also exiled South Africans, among them Bloke Modisane, who later wrote *Blame Me on History*; Lewis Nkosi,[5] who published articles in the London *Observer*; and Es'kia Mphahlele, the future author of *Down Second Avenue*, whom she would meet later in South Africa, where she taught for some years, and with whom she would retain a lifelong connection.

The Mbari club was to play a significant role in backing the now famous Makerere Conference of Writers of English Expression.

Molara O belongs squarely to that intellectual generation born under colonialism but coming of age at about the same time as much of Africa was emerging into nations. "Those were the days, my friend, we thought would never end," she recalled. "Days we thought Africa was walking into a new millennium of regeneration and reconstruction. . . ." It was a confidence most manifest in those writers gathered at Makerere in 1962. It was not that they were not critical of the emerging Africa, but their criticism was rooted in an optimism arising from the various opportunities opened by independence. We could see clearly our roles in the new dispensation: as critical visionaries and as builders of a new future and a new Africa that would not be a copy of the old Europe. The optimism was in the belief that there was now room for new critical visions. In short, our vision was nothing less than that of the new Man and Woman—the New African that Frantz Fanon would fantasize about in the last chapter of *The Wretched of the Earth*.

Pan-Africanism was part of those visions and part of the intellectual formation of that generation, who would come of age very aware of the life and work of the wide-ranging leaders of Black thought, from Marcus Garvey and George Padmore to W.E.B. Du Bois and Kwame Nkrumah.

Molara O has remained Pan-Africanist through and through. Her Pan-Africanism was not just the continentalism of Africa and African peoples and cultures, but also the world of Africana spanning the globe. It shaped her consciousness, and this can be seen in her work, with its roots in African, Caribbean, and African American history, politics, and culture. She married a Black Jamaican mathematician, the product of the University of Chicago and the Sorbonne, and has two Nigerian Jamaican daughters from the marriage. She has actively engaged with writers and intellectuals throughout Africa, including Okot p'Bitek,[6] Mbulelo Mzamane, Theo Luzuka, Dan Izevbaye, Felix Mnthali, Lewis Nkosi, and Mĩcere Mũgo. She also met Ama Ata Aidoo when they were both teenage undergraduates, Ama at the University of Ghana at Legon and Molara at the University of Ibadan. They met at a conference organized at the University of Ibadan by Langston Hughes.[7] She has given talks and taught in many parts of the continent, including South Africa, Mozambique, and Ghana. She speaks fondly of those lands as her own:

> I went to Mozambique by bus and train. You know those people's buses called *tro-tro* in Ghana, *matatu* in East Africa, and *danfo* in Nigeria. I went by one of these to Swaziland too, singing songs happily in the bus with the passengers to the driver's tape of Lionel Richie's love songs. I took those buses too when I was living in Umtata to sit among the people and listen to their broken

> English, as I did not speak Xhosa. Interesting how people can communicate across language disabilities. Some were saying what kind of professor is this. At the University of Mozambique I met scholars and experienced the movement of migrant labor to South Africa from surrounding African countries as Hugh Masekela's gripping jazz rendering of such train journeys had dramatized for me. What a beautiful seaside campus in that neglected city and capital of Mozambique with its Mediterranean architecture![8]

She takes delight in her work in African countries outside Nigeria. She is proud of her time in South Africa in what she describes as "the post-Mandela excitement" to help build a new South Africa: "That was 1996 to 1998 when the South African constitution was being written and I toured many of the universities then speaking on gender issues. That was when South Africa produced the most progressive constitution in the world today on gender."

At the University of Transkei, now Walter Sisulu University, she introduced new courses and founded a master's degree program. She also set up the first Gender Studies Center and degree.

That is Molara O, adventurous in life and thought.

What then is Ogundipe's place in African thought? Like other literary intellectuals of her generation, she was fed on the literary criticism that went with the study of English national literature, which meant the close reading of texts, with theory that was within the traditions of Coleridge, Matthew

Arnold, and F.R. Leavis. But even at Ibadan, her searching curiosity drove her beyond the confines of the purely formal and aesthetic to the sociology of literature. In 1969 she wrote on Amos Tutuola "to redeem him and to critique the wife of *The Palm-Wine Drinkard* as an ideal of Yoruba womanhood."[9] She also wrote pioneering essays on Okigbo and Achebe. In these early essays, she emphasized techniques of writing, the craft. She was interested in technique as discovery,[10] which she would later develop into a theory of narratology.

Molara O was among the earliest to bring a Marxist perspective to the study and analysis of the text and the wider culture of its making, and its reflection in the double sense of mimesis and evaluative contemplation. She told me she came to Marxism at Ibadan through international scholars, especially U.S.-educated Blacks and some Nigerians with anticolonial backgrounds and an education in Britain. She writes:

> You know one had heard about Marx, Engels, etc., and read Marxist literature at Ibadan through the English department, but it was, as you know, communicated in the manner of British conservatives, mocking, condescending and not-so-informed. It took my own later efforts to actually grasp the truths in Marx and Marxism and resolve the issues for Africa and myself to become finally a Marxist. A British lecturer said to me once: "Don't read Hegel, read Bertrand Russell." Of course, that impelled me to read Hegel!
>
> I was fascinated by a theory of history and society

> that was not religious or racist for I had been a daughter of Christian missionaries and very religious, looking for new interpretations of the world then. Historical materialism helped me think of Africa without racism and evaluate society anywhere as the product of human consciousness and skills.[11]

Her Marxist outlook has always been informed by critical feminist thought, which has its roots in her upbringing. When I asked her what came first, feminism or Marxism, she said feminism, but both had their roots in the education her mother instilled in her through books, stories, and by example: "Mama only made us love work; that is what provoked in me the attitude of respecting all labor. From there it was easy to embrace Marxist theory."

Feminism, too. As far back as she can recall, she remembers her mother advising "us women to make sure we can always support ourselves and our families and not depend totally on being maintained by men and be able to help our husbands as she did Papa; she insisted on our having professions as that was surest medicine against poverty."[12] Her gravitation to feminism was a logical and natural development from that foundation laid by her mother and their generation:

> They were not feminists, her generation, more like suffragettes who wanted the development of women in Nigeria and worked in the Women's section of pro-independence political parties.

Some of Molara O's most brilliant contributions to feminist thought came from her exchanges with her Malawian colleague and friend Felix Mnthali: "We had a very enriching intellectual interaction when we were at Ibadan. He arrived innocent of feminism when he came to Nigeria, where he made remarks to me to which I wrote a poem as rejoinder. He had a sense of humor about it, though he said everywhere he went feminists jumped up to challenge him all over again."

But the exchange generated more than a poem. It also produced probably the first major contribution to feminist theory and thought in Africa, informed by the Marxism of Marx, Lenin, and even Mao. The essay, "Not Spinning on the Axis of Maleness," was published by Doubleday in an anthology of essays from sixty-nine nations around the world that was edited by Robin Morgan, who was one of a group of 1960s American feminists, including Gloria Steinem, "now named the second generation by Western critics; that is, second to the British suffragettes."[13] The two-volume editions were titled: *Sisterhood Is Global*. Her essay thrust Molara O to the forefront of global feminist thought, and she certainly became one of the pioneers in feminist theory in Africa.

Molara O sees the oppression of women within the dialectical mutual affecting totality of the economy, politics, culture, and the psyche. For her, "the study of women must be done from a class perspective taking cognizance of class difference in all societies." In the particular case of Africa and the Black world, the oppression of Black women is deeply tied to the variables of race in the history of imperialism. Reacting to the simplistic view of feminism that all women are pitted against all men and therefore their struggle is an all-out war of all women against all men, she argues that the real enemy "is the total societal system, which is a jumble of neo-colonial and feudalistic, even slave-holding, structures and social attitudes."[14]

While rejecting the view that man is the enemy, she recognizes that "they become enemies when they seek to block these necessary historical changes; when for selfish power, they claim as their excuse 'culture and heritage'—as if human societies are not constructed by human beings; when they plead and laugh about the natural inferiority of women; when they argue that change is impossible because history is static—which it is not."

"Not Spinning on the Axis of Maleness" was published in 1984. "In some Nigerian critical historiography of Nigerian feminist historiography, the first published feminist text is usually named as my book, *Re-Creating Ourselves*, from 1994, but that is not so; it was this text."[15]

The book *Re-Creating Ourselves: African Women & Critical Transformations* is a fuller development of the theory first outlined in the classic essay "Not Spinning on the Axis of Maleness." But *Re-Creating Ourselves* has become a leading text in African thought, and it is used as a teaching text internationally, especially in the United States. The impact of Mao is clear in the book. Molara O freely acknowledges her admiration of his work:

> [I was] a fervent supporter, which has not changed despite the efforts to devalue his contribution and his very

> significant redemption of China from the clutches of imperialism. [I have] read him a lot and [have been] very influenced by his perceptions and methods, such as sending instructors to camps where they wrote self-evaluative essays to change themselves. I thought that had some deep ontological humor too apart from the intellectuality of the method. The Cultural Revolution was very important in the history and development of China, and we need some adaptations of that all over Africa today.

Not surprisingly, echoes of Mao are heard in her delineation of the six mountains that the African woman has to climb. The title is an expansion of Mao's four mountains on Chinese backs, but Molara O develops it to make it one of the most comprehensive statements on the status of woman in Africa, and by extension everywhere else.

I have always assigned the book, particularly the essay on the six mountains, in my literature classes. It helps illuminate the treatment of women in both male narratives like Ousmane Sembène's *God's Bits of Wood*, Achebe's *Things Fall Apart*, and Okot p'Bitek's *Song of Lawino*, as well as female narratives like Tsitsi Dangarembga's *Nervous Conditions*, Mariama Bâ's *So Long a Letter*, Nawal Saddawi's *Woman at Point Zero*, and Ngozi Adichie's *Half of a Yellow Sun*.

"There were African female theorists before me, but only in the social sciences and not Marxist," she wrote to me. "None in literature and literary theory to my knowledge."

Even her poetry is imbued with critical theory where emotion is thought and thought, emotion. Her place as a leader in dialectical feminism and criticism places her squarely as a leader of social thought. Her biography embodies that of postcolonial Africa. Sisterhood may be global, but for her it begins in Africa and is affected by all the variables of society: race, class, caste, sex and sexuality, and other forms of social stratification and division, such as physical disability. Despite setbacks, Molara O has never given up on Africa. In her life and work she continues to exude an optimism rooted in her belief that human societies are constructed by human beings and their skills, and that change is possible because history, like nature and thought, is not static.

Not surprisingly, transformation and liberation are key words in her outlook. In her 2007 book *Indigenous and Contemporary Gender Conception and Issues in Africa*, the terms are central to her definition of feminism as "a social philosophy that advocates and actively seeks the liberation and humanization of women in society." This book is important because, as she says, it brings her back to her lifelong interest in "indigenous concepts and constructions of human society and identities without which we cannot fully grasp the realities of African women, and men, or a correct understanding of the workings of African cultures." Appropriately, it is an African saying that sums up her dialectical, critical, and social outlook: I am human only because you are human.

Molara O concludes, "The liberation of women is a necessary condition for the liberation of men. And the liberation of both genders is the condition for the liberating the human."

It is more than a conclusion. It is a vision of tomorrow and could apply anywhere in our world today

20

The African Writer as a Prophet and Social Critic in Contemporary Times

It was in 1963 that Es'kia Mphahlele, then still in exile from the apartheid regime, founded the Chemchemi Creative Center in Nairobi. Kenya was on the verge of independence, but at the time, it was still a settler colony, a mirror image of apartheid South Africa. Chemchemi is the Swahili name for a spring or a fountain. It was meant to be a place where Kenyan writers could meet, to do for Kenya what the Mbari Writers Club, another of his creations, had done for Nigeria. At the time, there were hardly any published Kenyan writers to speak of. My own novel *Weep Not, Child*, the first in East Africa, had yet to be published. There must have been skeptical glances when this exile from South Africa set up this fountain for Kenyan writers, but no skepticism would deflect him from his purpose. Where others saw East Africa as a literary desert, Mphahlele saw fertile soil to plant seeds that would green the desert. He organized seminars at the center to which he invited budding and would-be writers. Mphahlele was focused on the future. The young were that future.

Apart from the seminars and activities at the CCC in Nairobi, Mphahlele traveled widely, talking at several schools. I'm sure there were many who saw him as a latter-day Don Quixote, mistaking shadows for writers. Like Don Quixote, Mphahlele stayed the course, oozing optimism even when results did not seem to give cause for it. Among the schools he visited in 1963 was Kamusinga high school in western Kenya, far from Nairobi. Among the students who attended the talk that day was a boy who sat in a corner quietly. He did not ask any questions. The boy had lost his father and was being brought up by a single mother. Maybe he was thinking about the hardships at home, imagining probably not a life of literature, but how his life might have been different were his father still alive. This boy would later become Dr. Henry Chakava, the CEO of East African Educational Publishers, the publishing house that he has run since the 1970s, developing it from a tiny house into a major publishing enterprise that has published many Kenyan and other African writers.

Mphahlele was not just a dreamer, but also a battle-tested activist and organizer. I first met him in Kampala, Uganda, during the 1962 Conference of Writers of English Expression. I was then a second-year student of English at Makerere. Mphahlele was the chief organizer and the brain behind the gathering. The contingent from East Africa had not published much beyond the occasional short story, in my case, in a student journal, and yet Mphahlele invited us and accorded us the full status of writers. I am forever beholden to him for enabling me to meet so many writers, many of whom had already published substantial work—books, essays, articles, poems, and short stories in significant literary journals and newspapers. Mphahlele built bridges among continental African writers, and a causeway between continental African writers and the African literary diaspora in the United States and the Caribbean. For me, he built stairs to the world of letters.

In a sense, Mphahlele has always been a bridge. The herdsboy from Maupaneng who became a scholar in Jo'burg would link the rural and the urban to produce one of the finest autobiographies, *Down Second Avenue*, which drew equally from his life and from his imagination in search of the truth of life in an oppressive social system. He deployed all the resources of a poet and a prose writer to meld historical fact and imaginative metaphor into lyrical tenderness. This would become his hallmark in his later works, for instance *The Wanderers* and *Africa My Music*, blurring the boundaries between writer, scholar, and educator, between writer and journalist, and between literary and social critic, as well as between genres—prose, poetry, and drama. It is not surprising that the author of the magnificent *Down Second Avenue* would also produce the groundbreaking work of literary criticism of the time *The African Image*, and later other collections of criticism, including *Es'kia*. As the fiction editor of *Drum* magazine in the 1950s, he was the link and mediating consciousness between the older generation of Krune Mqhayi, Wallet Vilakazi, the brothers Herbert and Rolfes Dhlomo, and Peter Abrahams, and the tough-minded urbanites Can Themba, Arthur Maimane, Lewis Nkosi, Bloke Modisane, Casey Motsisi, and Todd Matshikiza. The 1962 conference that linked South African writing to that of the African continent and Pan-Africanism as a whole was a continuation of the bridge he himself had become. Even if he had stopped at Makerere, Mphahlele would still have made an indelible mark on the African literary scene and its intellectual production.

He did not stop at creating platforms for writers. He also fought for the recognition of their work, of African literature, in the academy. He followed up the success of the Makerere conference with another at Fourah Bay College in Freetown, Sierra Leone. This time the conference focused on the place of African literature in the university. Was he discouraged by finding no immediate takers to his ideas on the teaching of African literature in the academy? He did not show it, because at Chemchemi he pushed and eventually was allowed to teach the first-ever course on African literature at Nairobi. With his departure for Zambia in 1966, the course was considerably diminished so that it became a virtual nonentity.

When, in 1967, I returned to Kenya from Leeds and joined the English Department of Nairobi University, I was confronted with the old English syllabus that I had studied as an undergraduate at Makerere. The department seemed impervious to the winds of literary change blowing within the continent. I joined two other colleagues to call for the abolition of the English Department as then organized.

The resulting change from the English Department to the Literature Department rested squarely on what Mphahlele had done. The seeds he had planted had grown and borne fruit in new departments of literature all over the continent and produced intellectuals that could match any from anywhere. Among the earliest takers of the reorganized literature syllabus was the boy who had once listened to Mphahlele speak to his class at Kamusinga, Dr. Henry Chakava.

Mphahlele was an intellectual activist who left a lasting mark on the production of Pan-African literature through the conferences he organized and the community centers he ran, like Chemchemi. Similarly, he left his mark through his campaigns for African literature in schools and colleges. His activism was deeply rooted in his commitment to education and the arts. He had already seen the arts play a role in his own life in the form of the stories and songs that nourished him as he contemplated the vastness of nature in the apparently endless plains and awe-inducing mountains and valleys. His activism was also based on his profound belief that the arts and artists had an indispensable role in society.

Mphahlele has written extensively about the role of literature and the writer in society. He believes that writers are both a mirror and the conscience of their society. They are the sensitive needle that registers the ugly and the beautiful, the negative and the positive, in all their interactions and their complexity. An excellent student of South African literary and intellectual history, Mphahelele was aware of the words of R.V. Selope Thema in an issue of the Chamber of Mines weekly newspaper for workers, *Umteteli wa Bantu* (Mouthpiece of the People), in March 1929:

> The duty of Bantu writers and journalists, as that of writers and journalists of other races, is to call the attention of the leaders to the things that are detrimental to the interest and welfare of our people. A writer who does

> not criticize and correct the mistakes of his people does not fulfill the purpose for which God endowed him with the power of the pen. A writer is a prophet, and his duty is not only to prophesy but also to rebuke, when necessary, the people for wrongdoing; to criticize, when occasion demands it, the conduct and methods of the leaders of his race, and point out the way of salvation.

The biblical prophets, for instance, would warn the rulers of their society about the wrath of God if they did not mend their ways. They spoke with anger precisely because they loved their society and wanted it to run with fairness and justice. Damnation was sure to descend on those rulers who would not hearken to the voice of the prophet. The prophet became the voice of the people.

This is still true in contemporary times. Writers have to be the voice of the voiceless. They have to give voice to silence, especially the silence imposed on a people by an oppressive state. The South African writer has played this role bravely and magnificently in the past, from Krune Mqhayi to Breyten Breytenbach. For their words alone, some of them have faced torture, exile, and death. Indeed, there were times when the South African writer, at home or in exile, was the most eloquent voice of the silenced. Some writers chose to engage in the very struggle they talked about in their books. They plunged into battle as actual fighters. Some died; others carried physical scars. History has seen many artists enter battle, like any other soldiers.

When one talks about the role of the writer or the arts, we

are referring to what they do with their pens, their brushes, their voices. One is not necessarily a good writer, a good painter, or a good singer for being a good soldier in the fight for liberation or a physical activist in social struggle. The biblical prophets would probably have made poor combatants in a battlefield. That is why I think it is dangerous to judge writers in terms of the parties and ideologies of their allegiance. One is not a poor or a good writer because one is in this or that party, or in this or that trade union. But the words a writer utters in song or story do matter, although not because they effect immediate change. A novel, for instance, takes years to complete, publish, and circulate. Changes cannot wait for the novelist to complete the novel or the poet the epic. The revolution will not wait for an inspiring tale.

What, then, is the real role of the artist and the arts in society? It is the part that the arts play in the very survival of the human. The human body needs food, water, and air to be. That is obvious. All life needs food, water, and air. But human beings have an ethical dimension to their being. Humans don't live to eat but eat to live. Humans make choices, moral and aesthetic, that create and cater to the spiritual dimension to their being. Many ethical systems in the form of religions and other ritual practices try to reflect and cater to this spirituality, to nourish the soul in the same way food nourishes the body. The body and the mind are essential to human existence.

However, there is one realm of our being without which there would be no difference between humans and the rest of nature. I am talking of the imagination. Imagination is central to the survival of humans as humans. Architects must picture a building in their minds before they can build it. Without imagination, there would be no religions. We imagine God and Satan as embodiments of the oppositional ideals of good and evil. Worship and ceremony would be impossible without imagination. Humans can imagine journeys before they set out on them. Humans can imagine the past and the future. We can imagine different futures, endless different possibilities, and then make choices based on what we imagine. This capacity to imagine a different future is important in order to resist succumbing to apparently impossible situations. We have seen how an oppressive social system, or rulers in general, try to limit our imagination, to make people unable to imagine and therefore struggle for a different future. That we have arrived at the best of all possible worlds is the constant refrain of the dominant social forces in society. Without imagination, there would be no songs, poetry, fiction, and prophecy.

Let us look at the three central constituents of a human being: the body, the soul, and the imagination. Humans make sure that they do not starve the body. They nourish it with enough healthy food where possible. Otherwise, the body shrivels, becomes weak. The same with spirituality. Humans nourish it with good ethical practices that ensure that they make good ethical choices and hold on to values that enhance their individual and collective lives. Religions, in the widest possible dimension of the term, cater to the spiritual to ensure that the "soul" does not shrivel because of bad advice, choices, and practices. They try to provide a healthy spiritual diet.

What about the imagination? What nourishes the imagination that is so central to our existence as humans? It is surely the arts. The imagination produces the food it needs for its nourishment, and this food is the arts. It is story, song, dance, sculpture, and painting. In his book on his sculptures, Pitika Ntuli says he started at the age of six when "I made my first sculpture with wire and discarded polish tins and my voice providing the revving sounds of the engine, hooting all the way to the shops." His imagination created a vehicle that in turn expanded the boy's imagination. His creation is a real vehicle in his imagination, and it empowers him.

Es'kia Mphahlele was very much aware of the centrality of imagination in society. He talked about the education of the imagination. "We invest words with the mystical power that can bring ramparts tumbling," he wrote, invoking the memory of Joshua's trumpet that brought down the walls of Jericho. "We speak with the tongues of prophets, priests, gurus," he adds, invoking the memory of myriads of prophets of all cultures and creeds, who, like Kwegyir Aggrey, ask the eagle to find its inner power and fly.[1]

The primary role of the writer, or more broadly the artist, is to produce the healthiest material for the education of the imagination. Just as unhealthy food weakens the body and bad ethical choices diminish the spiritual, so also bad art can limit the imagination or direct it to unhealthy ends. That's why the arts should not be a luxury in the school system. They should be central to it. Even engineers, architects, urban planners, teachers, and scientists thrive on a robust imagination that can find links between phenomena.

Es'kia Mphahlele inhabits several worlds. He was a writer who made other writers possible. His thinking and practice laid the grounds for the debates on the decolonization of literature and the formation of new kinds of literature departments. When we talk about the African writer as a prophet, an activist, and a social critic, we need go no further than the example of this man. In his life as an artist, educator, and activist, he truly embodies the voice of prophecy. Mphahlele started as a herdsboy listening and reciting stories. He became a teacher but was removed from teaching for his opposition to the Bantu Education Act, which extended apartheid throughout the educational system. He became a writer telling stories in *In Corner B*, published in 1967. The conditions in South Africa forced him into exile, to join the company of the Wanderers whom he talks about in his novel of the same title. For being an educator, a writer, and a defender of the arts, he was thrown out of the city into a wilderness that he would turn into a platform for his educational mission and literary prophecies.

Prophets are driven. They never give up dreams. Wherever he now rests, Mphahlele is maybe looking at us, telling us of his dreams as composed by the poet Langston Hughes, whom Mphahlele brought to Makerere and with whom, as with other Black writers, he continued his literary conversations from his beginnings as a short story writer to his days at Denver and Jo'burg.

To fling my arms wide
In some place of the sun,
To whirl and to dance

Till the white day is done.
Then rest at cool evening
Beneath a tall tree
While night comes on gently,
Dark like me—
That is my dream!

To fling my arms wide
In the face of the sun.
Dance! Whirl! Whirl!
Till the day is done.
Rest at pale evening . . .
A tall, slim tree . . .
Night coming tenderly
Black like me.

Those dreams of freedom reunite us with the spirit of Mphahlele, the exile, who never stopped dreaming of home.

Notes

1: Decolonizing Education

Keynote address at the Second ForumBIE 2030 organized by the Education Relief Foundation, in Mexico City, Mexico, November 21, 2018.

1 Walter Rodney, *How Europe Underdeveloped Africa* (1972; rev. ed., Baltimore, MD: Black Classic Press, 2011), 259.

2 This account was part of the testimony by a Maori politician, Dover Samuels, that I recently saw quoted by the Radio New Zealand (RNZ) website, September 2015. This took me back to my encounter with the young Maori woman in 1984.

2: The Body of Knowledge

KCA University lecture, Nairobi, Kenya, 2016.

3: Between Enslavement and Empowerment

1 David Kimble, *A Political History of Ghana* (Oxford, U.K.: Oxford University Press, 1963), 518.

2 A.G. Hoplins, "R.B. Blaize: Merchant Prince of West Africa," *Tarikh* 1, no. 2 (1966).

4: The Magic Fountain

The Ashby Lecture, at Clare Hall, Cambridge, U.K., May 1999. I would like to thank Toral Gajarawala for her research input into this paper.

1 I finished it as Distinguished Professor of English and Comparative Literature at the University of California–Irvine.

2 Although it did not work out, I was excited at the possibility for mutual exchange among such journals making possible through translations a genuine dialogue among African languages.

3 The conference, "Against All Odds," later came up with the Asmara Declaration on African Languages and Literatures.

5: The Modern Patron: The Role of the University in a Global Community

Paper read at the Inauguration Symposium, "The University and Society in the 21st Century," Honoring Chancellor Michael V. Drake as Fifth Chancellor of the University of California–Irvine, April 6, 2006.

6: Makerere Dreams

Speech given at the program for the University of East Africa fiftieth-anniversary celebrations on June 29, 2013, Main Hall, Makerere University, Kampala, Uganda.

7: Abdilatif Abdalla and the Voice of Prophecy

Plenary speech at the symposium, " 'Deep Language Crossing Borders': Exploring the Use of Culture as Resource in Political Activism and Resistance in Africa and Elsewhere," University of Leipzig, Germany, May 5, 2011, on the occasion of the retirement of Abdilatif Abdalla from the University of Leipzig.

1 Translated into English as *I Will Marry When I Want*, the play was written by Ngũgĩ wa Thiong'o and Ngũgĩ wa Mĩriĩ. Its performance was banned by the Kenya government on November 16, 1977.

10: Mazrui and Achebe: The Literary Artist and the Political Scientist

Presented at the thirty-eighth annual conference of the New York African Studies Association on June 6, 2013, at Bingham University, Karu, Nigeria, in a plenary conversation in memory of Chinua Achebe.

12: Mĩcere Mũgo: In Kenyan History, Literature, and Thought

Plenary talk at the "Tireless Pursuit: Celebration of the Life and Work of Mĩcere Mũgo," Syracuse University, Thursday, April 2, 2015.

1 European imperialism is characterized by settler colonies, including South and North America, Australia, and New Zealand.
2 Frantz Fanon, *The Wretched of the Earth*, trans. Constance Farrington (New York: Grove Press, 1965), 166.

15: The Three Js: Jomo, Jaramogi, and "James"

Remarks at a meeting of Kenyans held at California State University–Los Angeles to welcome His Excellency Raila Odinga, Kenya's prime minister, on his first visit to Los Angeles, April 17, 2011. Over four hundred Kenyans and other Africans attended the meeting.

16: Mandela Memories: An African Prometheus

Parts of this article have been published in *The Standard* (Kenya) and the *Sunday Independent* (South Africa).
1 For more on Kamĩrĩthũ, see my books *Decolonizing the Mind* and *Detained: A Writer's Prison Diary*.

19: Call Her Molara O: Pioneer in Dialectical African Feminism

1 Personal communication.
2 Email, June 20, 2016.
3 Banham's email to me, July 4, 2016.
4 Personal communication.
5 Nkosi, Modisane, and even Mphahlele, along with Can Themba and Todd Matshikiza, were among those who wrote for the popular South African *Drum* magazine.
6 Molara O wrote her PhD thesis for Leiden University on a narratological, dialectical, and feminist reading of Okot p'Bitek's *Song of Lawino*.
7 According to Molara O, little did they know, till later, that they were sitting with the literary genius of the Harlem Renassance.
8 Email, June 22, 2016.
9 Personal notes to me.
10 Personal note.
11 Email, June 22, 2016.
12 Personal commnication.
13 Personal communication.

14 *Sisterhood Is Global: The International Women's Movement Anthology* (New York: Doubleday, 1984), p. 503.
15 Email, July 8, 2016.

20: The African Writer as a Prophet and Social Critic in Contemporary Times

The First Annual Es'kia Mphahlele Memorial Lecture, sponsored by UNISA and given at Polokwane, Limpopo, South Africa, on August 25, 2010.

1 Kwegyir Aggrey, from Ghana, then Gold Coast, was a member of the Phelps-Stokes Commission on Education, which visited South Africa and East Africa in the twenties of the previous century. He used to tell the story of a farmer who had brought up an eagle to think of itself as a chicken because it was raised in the farmer's flock. A hunter passes by and claims that he can make the eagle fly, to the skepticism of the farmer. The hunter fails twice but does not give up, and eventually succeeds in making the eagle find its eaglitude.

About the Author

One of the leading writers and scholars at work today, **Ngũgĩ wa Thiong'o** was born in Limuru, Kenya, in 1938. He is the author of *A Grain of Wheat*; *Weep Not, Child*; and *Petals of Blood*, as well as *Birth of a Dream Weaver*, *Wrestling with the Devil*, *Minutes of Glory*, and *The Perfect Nine* (all from The New Press). Currently Distinguished Professor of English and Comparative Literature at the University of California–Irvine, Ngũgĩ is the recipient of twelve honorary doctorates, among other awards, and has been nominated for the Man Booker International Prize.

Publishing in the Public Interest

Thank you for reading this book published by The New Press; we hope you enjoyed it. New Press books and authors play a crucial role in sparking conversations about the key political and social issues of our day.

We hope that you will stay in touch with us. Here are a few ways to keep up to date with our books, events, and the issues we cover:

- Sign up at www.thenewpress.com/subscribe to receive updates on New Press authors and issues and to be notified about local events
- www.facebook.com/newpressbooks
- www.x.com/thenewpress
- www.instagram.com/thenewpress

Please consider buying New Press books not only for yourself, but also for friends and family and to donate to schools, libraries, community centers, prison libraries, and other organizations involved with the issues our authors write about.

The New Press is a 501(c)(3) nonprofit organization; if you wish to support our work with a tax-deductible gift please visit www.thenewpress.com/donate or use the QR code below.